TIME BANDITS

In the pitch darkness, Kevin [illegible] rch in one ha[illegible] his time the[illegible] no nothing. E[illegible] ry normal. [illegible] le staying aw[illegible] ds the wardro[illegible] ng back from [illegible] the hall light go out and heard the door to his parent's room close. All was silent, and his head began to drop again. Somewhere a clock chimed one. Finally against his will, Kevin fell asleep, but no sooner had his eyes closed than a single, heavy THUD from the wardrobe snapped him wide awake.

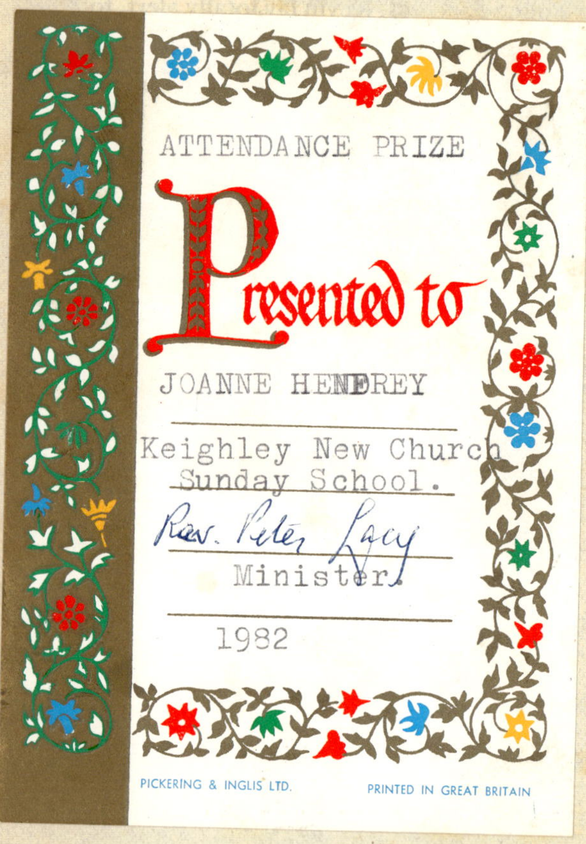
ATTENDANCE PRIZE

Presented to

JOANNE HENDREY

Keighley New Church
Sunday School.

Rev. Peter Lacy
Minister.

1982

PICKERING & INGLIS LTD.   PRINTED IN GREAT BRITAIN

TIME BANDITS

CHARLES ALVERSON

BASED ON A SCREENPLAY BY
MICHAEL PALIN
AND
TERRY GILLIAM

A Sparrow Book
Published by Arrow Books Limited
3 Fitzroy Square, London W1P 6JD

An imprint of the Hutchinson Publishing Group

London Melbourne Sydney Auckland
Wellington Johannesburg and agencies
throughout the world

First published 1981

Reprinted 1981

Set in Times
by Book Economy Services, Cuckfield, Sussex

Made and printed in Great Britain
by The Anchor Press Ltd

ISBN 0 09 926020 4

CONTENTS

—1—
THE KNIGHT IN THE WARDROBE

Supper!'

His mother's penetrating voice cut in just as Kevin was in the middle of a very important battle. Kneeling in the corner of his bedroom in a house in a new suburb of south-east London, Kevin Lotterby was masterminding a shoot-out between his tribe of plastic Comanche Indians and an interstellar battletank complete with laser cannon.

Kevin, a slightly scruffy boy of eleven, with a round, cheerful face, was providing both the shrill Comanche war-cries and the hissing boom of the cannons. But even through the noise of battle, his mother's voice cut in as relentlessly as a stainless steel buzzsaw.

'Kevin! Supper!'

'All *right*!' Kevin called reluctantly, throwing a sortie of mounted knights into the unequal fight against the battletank. 'Zam! Pow!' the laser cannon cut a wide hole in their armoured ranks. The rest of the knights and Comanches hurled themselves recklessly at their modern foe.

'Kevin! I'm not calling you again!'

'Okay, okay, I'm coming,' Kevin muttered, getting up and looking down on the epic battleground. Then, with one well-aimed sweep of his right foot, he ended the battle completely before picking up a thick book called *Heroes of Ancient Greece* and heading downstairs to supper.

Kevin's father was sitting at the new eating bar/counter

reading the evening paper while his mother, a neat blonde woman, bustled around in a kitchen bristling with gleaming, chromium-plated gadgets designed for the trouble-free preparation and cooking of food. As Kevin seated himself next to his father, there was a loud ping from one of the machines.

Mrs Lotterby opened the oven door and took out three identical aluminium-foil containers. Ripping off the tops of the containers, she sat two of them down before Kevin and his father. Mr Lotterby immediately began eating, his face still hidden behind his newspaper, but Kevin, who'd been reading about Agamemnon, legendary King of Mycenae in ancient Greece, looked up with a puzzled expression.

'What's this?' he asked.

Mrs Lotterby picked up one of the shiny packages and read from its side: 'Chicken creole, duchesse potatoes, carrots Vichy . . .' When Kevin looked doubtful, she added: 'It says here that it's lovely.'

Kevin didn't look convinced. 'Which one is the chicken?' he asked, looking glumly at three seemingly identical mounds on the serving tray.

With irritation, Mrs Lotterby said, 'Er . . . it's the one on the left. Now, be quiet and eat it.'

Kevin picked at the mound which was supposed to be chicken and began reading again.

Throwing the container down, Mrs Lotterby said with exasperation: 'What we need is something to take these things out of the packet automatically. It's wearing me out – all this unwrapping. . . .'

'We can't have everything, dear,' said Kevin's father from behind his newspaper.

'Why ever not?' Mrs Lotterby demanded. 'I know some people who have.' She, too, sat down and began to eat.

After supper, Mr and Mrs Lotterby were sitting in front of the king-sized, remote-controlled colour television set, leafing through mail-order catalogues, while Kevin sat in a far corner lost in his book about Greek heroes.

An enthusiastic voice on the television was booming: 'Yes, folks . . . Moderna Designs present the latest in kitchen luxury . . . the Moderna Wonder Major All-Automatic Convenience Centre-ette. It gives you all the time in the world to do all the things you really want to do!'

Mr and Mrs Lotterby, sitting staring at the screen, started as Kevin looked up and said: 'Dad? Did you know that ancient Greek warriors had to learn forty-four different ways of unarmed combat?'

But his parents were in another world as the announcer continued: '. . . A washing machine that cleans, dries, irons and tells you the time and temperature in twenty-six different international capitals. And an infra-red freezer-oven complex that can make you a meal from packet to plate in fifteen and a half seconds flat!'

'The Morrisons' can do it in only eight seconds,' Mrs Lotterbye said. 'Block of ice to bœuf Bourgignon in eight seconds. Lucky things!'

Kevin insisted from the corner: 'Did you know that the ancient Greeks could kill people in twenty-six different ways?'

'Bedtime for you, Kevin,' said his father without turning around. 'It's nine o'clock.'

'And this King Agamemnon,' Kevin went on, 'he once fought. . . .'

'Go on, dear,' Kevin's mother cut in shrilly, 'do what your father said!'

'Oh, all right,' said Kevin, picking up his book and trudging up the open-plan stairs as the television droned behind him. Halfway up the stairs he stopped and turned: 'Dad, do you think we could go to Greece one day?'

'Good night!' his parents chorused without taking their eyes from the big, flickering screen. Kevin turned and began walking again.

On the television, the compère was saying: 'Well, that's

today's star prize, so let's meet today's star guests on 'Your Money Or Your Life!' "

Up in his room, which he had made his own as much as possible by sticking clippings from books and magazines on the walls, Kevin put on his pyjamas and started to get into bed. But first he paused at the massed battle he'd been waging and added to the fray a couple of Napoleonic hussars mounted on chargers. Then, clutching his book, he climbed into bed and began reading once more about Agamemnon.

'And turn that light off!' came his father's voice from downstairs.

'It *is* off,' shouted Kevin. He turned the bedside lamp off with a sigh and snuggled down into his bedding. The noise from the television downstairs seemed to recede into a blanket of silence. Then, just as Kevin's eyelids were closing, a strange and violent clanking and banging began to come from the wardrobe standing opposite his bed. It was not like any noise he'd ever heard. It was distant yet very near. A rumbling, thundering roar.

Kevin sat up in bed and peered anxiously into the darkness. The noises got louder. Suddenly, before his very eyes, the wardrobe doors burst open – splinters flying everywhere – and a medieval knight in full armour on horseback charged out of the wardrobe and into the bedroom. His thick-chested mount was covered in sweat and froth.

As Kevin stared wide-eyed, the knight, brandishing a huge sword and shouting violently, swerved the horse around in the bedroom, knocking furniture and toys about wildly in a swirling gust of wind and dried leaves. Kevin dodged as the blade of the great sword swooped, knocking the bedside lamp into a corner. Then suddenly, with a wild cry from the knight, the battlehorse gathered his strength and leaped straight over Kevin's bed. Kevin was amazed to see him charge down a darkened avenue of tall trees which had magically appeared where a wall used to be and gallop away into the distance with a dying thump of hoofbeats.

Kevin slowly and wonderingly poked his head out from under the bedclothes and looked around his room. Everything had returned to normal: the wardrobe doors were intact and snugly closed; there was no damage, no mess, no knight, and a very ordinary wall where the avenue of trees had been. Warily, Kevin crept out of bed and turned on the bedside lamp which was back in its place undamaged. He went over to the wall through which the knight had vanished. It certainly felt real. There was nothing strange . . . except . . . there pinned on the wall was a magazine photograph of an avenue of trees *exactly* like the one down which the knight had disappeared.

Kevin spun round as the door to his room was suddenly thrown open, and his father appeared angrily in the doorway. 'What on earth is going on up here?' Mr Lotterby demanded. 'I told you to turn that light off and get to bed. And *no* more noise.'

The door slammed shut as Kevin turned back to his bed. It took him quite a while to get to sleep.

—2—

ENTER THE TIME BANDITS

The next night, Kevin was once again sitting at supper with his mother and father, but it would have been obvious to anyone that he was anxious to be somewhere else.

'Mum . . .' he began eagerly.

His mother turned on him half angrily: 'And you're going to bed in good time tonight, too!'

'Actually,' Kevin said, 'I was thinking that I'd go to bed right *now* if . . .'

'Now?' said his mother. 'Certainly not!'

'You must wait until your food's gone down,' his father said.

'But I haven't eaten anything,' Kevin said.

'Well, you *must* eat your food,' his mother insisted.

'And *then* wait for it to go down,' Mr Lotterby added. 'I always. . .'

But he was cut short by a shrill whining sound and a series of rapid buzzes from an alarm. Across the kitchen, a shiny machine suddenly began slicing meat and throwing the bits halfway across the room.

'Oh, no,' cried Mrs Lotterby, 'not the carvery again,' as she rushed to try to stop the torrent of fresh-cut ham.

Later, his parents were once again planted in front of the television watching a quiz show – with lavish, modern, automated, time-saving prizes – when Kevin told them: 'It's gone down now . . . my supper . . . I can feel it. Can I go to bed, please?'

'All right,' said his father without looking away from the set. 'Off you go . . . but no noise!'

'Good night, dear,' said his mother absently.

This time, up in his room, Kevin did not dawdle on the way to bed. Neither did he undress. Putting a torch and a Polaroid instant camera into his leather school satchel, he pulled his dressing gown over his clothes and jumped into bed fully dressed with the satchel in his arms. Whatever strange and weird thing was going to happen in his room tonight, he wasn't going to miss it. Eagerly but hesitantly, he turned out the light.

In the pitch darkness, Kevin lay totally alert, torch in one hand, instant camera in the other. But this time there was no rattling, no clanking, no nothing. Everything in his room was normal. Very normal. And soon Kevin was having trouble staying awake. Idly, he flashed his torch towards the wardrobe, but he saw nothing. Later, jerking back from half sleep, Kevin noticed the hall light go out and heard the door to his parents' room close. All was silent, and his head began to droop again. Somewhere a clock chimed one.

Finally against his will, Kevin fell asleep. No sooner had his eyes closed than a single, heavy THUD! from the wardrobe snapped him wide awake. Then came a series of very rapid heavy thumps, followed by muffled curses and apparently human grunts and groans. Kevin felt a cold shiver run up his spine. Cautiously he pulled himself up on his elbows, took the torch from his satchel and pointed it but did not turn it on. He shuddered as he heard the wardrobe door creak open in the dark, and then a babble of voices.

'Where are we?'

'I don't know.'

'Look at the map.'

'It's not *on* the map.'

'Is He coming after us?'

'Don't panic.'

'*Is* He coming after us?'

Kevin stretched his finger towards the switch on the torch as a voice said: 'I don't know. I think we gave Him the slip.'

Then Kevin pushed the switch, and the powerful beam of the torch captured a group of six dwarves dressed in a motley assortment of costumes each from a different era of history. They all stared into the light of the torch fearfully. As Kevin was shortly to find out, their names were Randall, Strutter, Wally, Og, Fidgit and Vermin.

Og, the one in a Viking helmet with only one horn and a scarlet waistcoat, cried with fright: 'It's Him!'

The six little men tried to get away from the light. Like frightened animals, they rushed back and forth along the wall of the bedroom.

'He's found us,' moaned Strutter, who was dressed in an Elizabethan doublet, gold-rimmed granny glasses and a brown, square-topped bowler hat.

'We're done for,' Wally, who wore a pirate's hat with a real monkey's skull and crossed bones, exclaimed.

'I told you so!' Fidgit protested. Fidgit wore a vegetable colander with a candle on it, British Army camouflage trousers and spats.

'We've had it,' Strutter said with resignation.

Finally, after all rushing about like mad things, the dwarves ended up in a whimpering heap in the farthest corner of Kevin's bedroom. Randall, dressed in a Scottish regimental dress jacket and wearing a World War Two leather flying helmet with earflaps, whispered to the others: 'Leave it to me.' A monocle on a golden chain glittered in his right eye. If the dwarves had a natural leader it was Randall. But only just.

Stepping hesitantly forward in the glare of the torch and clutching an ancient parchment map covered with strange symbols, Randall addressed the unseen enemy deferentially: 'We can explain everything, sir . . . honestly! We only borrowed it, you see, sir . . . and then we were . . . er . . .

so happy, that we just ran off . . . sort of . . . in high – uh – spirits. We were on our way back, actually, when. . .'

Finally, Kevin could contain himself no longer. 'Who are you, please?' he asked.

Suddenly, the dwarves were transformed. No longer were they cowering, whimpering beings. Instantly they bristled with suspicion, even outrage.

'That's not *Him*!' Strutter proclaimed.

'Doesn't sound like Him,' agreed Fidgit.

'Doesn't look like Him either,' said Wally, his eyes getting used to the light.

'It *isn't* Him,' announced Strutter, straightening his bowler.

'Right,' commanded Randall, suddenly very angry. 'Come on! Let's get him.'

Before Kevin could even move, the dwarves as one man leapt across the room and on to the bed. Randall jumped across Kevin's chest, issuing orders to the others. Kevin, frightened, struggled with these strange little men, and all was confusion.

'Ow! My nose!' Wally cried, as a boot connected with it.

'Help him,' Randall ordered. 'Og! Help him.'

'Help *who*?' Og wondered, trying to keep the Viking helmet from slipping over his eyes.

'*Him*!' Randall commanded. 'Wally! Right, gang, get one leg each and. . .'

In the struggle, Kevin and the little men fell off the bed in a heap of bedclothes, and Kevin ended up on the bottom, pinned to the floor by several of the dwarves.

'Strutter,' ordered Randall, 'get the torch.' Strutter obeyed, and soon a strong beam of light was shining in Kevin's face as he lay struggling with the strange invaders.

'It's only a kid!' Strutter exclaimed.

Taking immediate charge, Randall snapped: 'Og! Fidgit! Check the door.' The two leapt up and dashed for the door. Fidgit jumped on Og's shoulders and looked out through the clear glass light above the door.

'All clear!' he called.

Meanwhile, Strutter had put the bedside lamp back up on the table and switched it on. Randall pulled Kevin to his feet with short but powerful arms. 'Right!' he said, sticking his face up to Kevin's. 'Listen to me. Help us get out of here, and you won't get hurt.'

'Much,' added Wally menacingly from behind Randall.

Kevin, stuttering with amazement, said 'Why–w–why don't you just get out the way you came in?'

Grabbing Kevin by the pyjama front, Randall snarled: 'Don't try to be smart, you *little* creep.'

'Little cleverdick! Smartydrawers!' muttered the others.

'If you want to play it smart,' threatened Randall, 'I'll introduce you to Vermin here.' He nodded towards a little man who looked a lot like a walking refuse heap topped with a Confederate forage cap from the American Civil war. 'He eats anything, you know. Especially bits of people he doesn't like.'

'And I don't think he likes *you*,' Wally added.

Kevin began to try to back away. 'I'm not trying to be smart,' he insisted. 'I'm just trying to help.'

'You know, don't you?' Randall insisted, following Kevin nearer the wall.

'I don't know anything,' said Kevin, still backing.

'You know, and you're not going to tell us,' Randall growled. 'And *I'm* getting angry.'

'But . . .' said Kevin, his shoulders flat against the wall.

'And Vermin's getting hungry!'

The hungry look on Vermin's face startled Kevin. 'Aargh!' he exclaimed as the wall he was pressed against suddenly moved back as Randall lunged toward him. Kevin fell to the floor in amazement. The wall of his room, bookshelves, bulletin board and all, had moved back at least two feet.

'He's found it! He's found it!' Randall shouted.

'What?' said Strutter in confusion.

'The way out,' explained Randall jubilantly.

'It's never done *that* before,' said Kevin with puzzlement and he picked himself up, pushing at the wall gingerly with one hand. It seemed to move slightly under the pressure.

'Here,' said Randall, handing Kevin back his torch, 'hold this.' To the others he shouted: 'Come on, you lot . . . push!'

The six dwarves rushed to the movable wall and began to push, but the first three pushed so hard that the wall shot away from them, and the other three fell to the floor.

'Come on,' pleaded Randall. 'Let's do this as a team! Wait for me to give the order. Right! Ready . . .'

They all leaned against the wall while Kevin looked on in wonder.

'One . . .' cried Randall. Og and Vermin began pushing at once, tumbling the other four in a heap.

'Wait!' implored Randall. "Whoever heard of anybody starting at "one"? I'll say "One-two-three" and then we'll all heave.'

'We heave on two?' asked Og, 'or is it three?'

'Three!' said Randall with exasperation, and half of them started pushing madly, knocking the other three down again, but pushing the wall about five feet from where it started. Randall was about to get angry once more when suddenly there was the *whooshing* sound of a great wind, and Kevin's torch was obscured in an ultra-bright light, a spectral radiance, from behind them.

'He's found us!' Wally cried.

'Who?' Kevin asked.

'Him!' Og said.

'Heave! heave!' cried Randall urgently. 'One-two-three! One-two-three!'

All six put their shoulders to the wall and pushed. The wall began to move steadily, but not fast enough. 'Help us,' Randall begged Kevin. 'Please . . . help us.'

Kevin didn't know *what* to do. He wasn't sure that he *wanted* to help these strange men. But as the rushing wind and the strange light grew closer, Kevin made up his mind that any adventure was better than none and began to push with all his strength. The wall really began to move, and Randall cried: 'That's it! Push!'

Ten . . . thirty . . . fifty feet the wall moved. With all seven pushing furiously, the bedroom took the shape of a long corridor as they left Kevin's bed, dresser and other furnishings in the distance. Behind them the glow turned into a brilliant white figure with a long beard and a mane of hair like a lion's. The wind howled, swirling his hair and long robes majestically, as the figure pursued them down the lengthening corridor.

'Push!' cried Randall frantically.

'Who is *that*?' Kevin couldn't help asking even as he pushed with all his might.

'*Push!*' repeated Randall, but as hard as they pushed the figure chasing them kept getting closer, pointing at them with a long, accusing finger.

'Stop!' cried the mysterious figure. 'Return what you have stolen from me. Return . . . return . . . return the map or it will bring you great danger. Stop! . . . NOW!'

But the dwarves and Kevin were pushing so madly, so blindly, that they couldn't stop. Suddenly they lost their balance as the wall dropped away into darkness, and they fell after it into the blackness of space.

'Heelllp!' their voices cried and then faded as the seven of them tumbled endlessly through the inky, boundless void. High behind them in the tiny square of light which was Kevin's bedroom, the ghostly figure stood watching them with glowing eyes as they fell, their figures distorting, stretching and twisting and re-forming as they passed through galaxies of black spheres in even blacker space.

Kevin, as amazed as he was frightened, wondered where he was falling to and whether their descent would ever end.

—3—

BACKWARDS IN TIME

In a deserted, dusty farmyard, a lone, skinny chicken was pecking listlessly at a worm when suddenly the sun was blotted out by the plummeting bodies of six dwarves and an eleven-year-old boy. As the squawking chicken escaped, six of the figures landed in a mixed-up heap on the spot where it had been pecking, and the seventh, Og, splashed into a nearby water trough with a mighty sploosh. Wasting no time, the dwarves jumped up and dashed for a nearby barn, dragging with them Kevin still clutching his school satchel. As one man, they dived head first into a pile of straw, totally disappearing from sight.

'What's going . . .' Kevin tried to ask, but Strutter clamped his hand over the boy's mouth. Randall peered nervously from the straw to the place where they landed. After a few tense moments, he let out a sigh of relief.

'Whew . . . that was close,' Randall announced. 'All clear.'

'Slowly the others began to appear from their hiding places. Strutter let Kevin go, and the dwarves brushed the straw from their clothes, looking as if they had survived a very close thing. It took Wally some time to find his pirate's hat.

'Who *are* you?' Kevin demanded, annoyance getting the better of his fear.

'Shhh!' said Randall impatiently.

'Where are we?' Kevin insisted. 'What happened to my room? Who was that awful man? Why did he want to. . .'

'That was no man,' said Fidgit, who Kevin thought looked like the nicest of the dwarves. 'That was the Supreme Being.'

'You mean – God?' asked Kevin wonderingly.

'We never got to know him *that* well,' said Fidgit. 'We only worked for Him. . .'

'Shaddap!' said Randall. 'Are we all here?' He looked around, counting his disreputable followers. 'Wally . . . Strutter . . . Og . . . Fidgit . . .' he called the roll until he came to Vermin. 'Vermin,' repeated Randall, but there was no answer. 'Vermin!'

Then a grunt came from a dark corner of the barn behind some bales, and Vermin emerged from hiding with a shy secretive smile and chicken feathers around his sharp-toothed little mouth. He was hiding something behind his back.

'Will you *stop* eating?' demanded Randall.

'I'd rather he ate *them* than us,' said Wally, who had once been bitten by Vermin.

'Right,' said Randall, 'it's not safe to stay here, so long as *He* is still after us, so we've got to keep moving. Og, you and Vermin. . .'

Suddenly Kevin, seeing his chance to escape, made a break for it and dashed out of the barn into the bright sunshine. He didn't know where he was going, but it seemed better than hanging around with a bunch of crazy, and possibly dangerous, dwarves.

'Hey,' he heard Randall's voice from inside the barn, 'after him. He'll give us all away!'

With his longer legs, Kevin was able to sprint across the barnyard and down a slope before the dwarves could get out of the barn. Jumping over a small stream, he pushed into some thick shrubbery and, hidden from view, looked back to see the dwarves at the top of the slope looking in all directions. Plunging on through a small copse of trees, Kevin found himself in the clear again and approaching a dirt road. All around was open country. It didn't look like any countryside he'd ever seen.

Suddenly he stopped. All at once he recognized his surroundings. He was standing in the middle of two rows of trees – the same broad avenue of elms down which the knight from his wardrobe had disappeared. Kevin stood dumbfounded.

But his wonderment was cut short by the thundering of hooves immediately behind him. Spinning around, Kevin was nearly trampled underfoot by three madly galloping horses ridden by soldiers wearing the tight tunics, shakos and epaulettes of eighteenth-century French hussars. The horses reared, nearly out of control, to miss the gaping boy.

'Dammit, boy,' cried the lead hussar, trying to rein in his mount, 'these horses are valuable!'

The second hussar drew his curved sabre and flourished it at Kevin. 'You little fool!' The sharp blade missed Kevin by inches.

'Leave him,' shouted the third hussar. 'We're late!'

The three hussars wheeled their spirited mounts and rode off over the hill as Kevin stared openmouthed at this coming to life of his favourite toys. Then he began to run up the hill after the dashing hussars. 'Wait!' he cried.

By the time Kevin reached the brow of the hill, the hussars and their mounts were gone. He stopped. His jaw dropped in amazement. There spread out before his eyes was a sweeping panorama of a late-eighteenth-century battlefield: the dead, the wounded, the overturned cannon, and all the confusion of a bitter struggle. And in the distance, surrounded by fiercely fighting troops, was a walled city, now burning fiercely. Refugees streamed out of the city towards Kevin, and he was soon caught up in the chaos of fleeing civilians and wounded soldiers on foot and in wagons. A hurrying refugee bumped into Kevin, knocking him down.

'On your feet, boy,' said the refugee, an old man with a

crudely bandaged head wound. He helped Kevin up.

'Get a move on,' cried a monk driving a cartload of weeping nuns. 'They're taking prisoners.'

'Excuse me,' Kevin asked politely, 'what town is this?'

'Castiglione,' said a limping merchant, adding bitterly, 'or what Napoleon's left of it.'

'Napoleon?' Kevin said, stopping in his tracks. 'Napoleon Bonaparte?'

'That's right,' said the merchant, 'the devil himself. It's *his* city now.' He spat on the rich, red earth. 'Come on, boy,' he told Kevin, 'you'll come with us, if you know what's good for you.'

'Thanks, but I have to . . .' Kevin said, trying to thread his way against the tide of refugees. 'Napoleon!' he said to himself in wonder.

'You're going the wrong way!' screamed an old woman, vainly trying to keep her many petticoats out of the thick dust on the road.

Meanwhile, Randall and the others, having given up hope of finding Kevin, were crouched underneath a bridge over which refugees' carts were constantly rumbling. They were studying an ancient map.

'Now,' Randall was saying, 'we obviously went a little wrong when we ended up in that brat's bedroom, but don't worry, I'll get you out of this.'

'The map's upside down,' Strutter pointed out.

'Listen,' Randall demanded angrily, 'do you want to run this gang?'

'Oh, no . . . no,' Strutter exclaimed. 'We agreed . . . no leader.'

'Right,' said Randall, 'so shut up and do as I say.' He lowered his eyes to the map, quickly turning it the right way up.

Kevin was trying to push his way over the bridge, fighting his way against the human traffic, when a huge ox-cart veered towards him, forcing him to vault over the side of the bridge. He tumbled down the river embankment, ending up in the midst of the scheming dwarves.

'You!' said Randall accusingly.

'Where did you go to?' asked Fidgit.

Kevin couldn't honestly say that he was glad to see the strange dwarves again, but he certainly had something to tell them. 'Do you know where we *are*?' he exclaimed.

'Shut up,' Randall exclaimed, grabbing Kevin and pulling him down beneath the bridge. He pointed a stubby finger at the sky. 'If the Supreme Being finds us, he'll turn us all into used handkerchiefs, just like that.' He snapped his fingers noisily.

'I'm sorry,' Kevin whispered, 'but . . . I mean . . . this is the year 1796; that burning city is Castiglione . . . and those are the troops of Napoleon Bonaparte!'

The dwarves all looked at each other. 'Isn't this where we were *meant* to be?' asked Strutter.

Randall took a close look at the map. 'That's right,' he said. '1796 . . . Castiglione . . . Northern Italy.'

'How did you know *that*?' Wally exclaimed, looking at Kevin with new respect.

'Oh,' said Kevin modestly. 'It was nothing.' In fact, he'd read about the battle in one of his history books.

'That's very good,' said Strutter.

'*Very* good,' said Fidgit. 'What *else* do y'know?'

'All right, all right,' said Randall crossly. 'You can get his autograph later.' To Kevin, he said, 'By the way, what's your name?'

'Kevin. Kevin Lotterby.'

'Right, Kevin,' said Randall, 'now you shut up and play your cards right, and we could make you a very rich man. Fidgit, you keep a close eye on him.' Turning back to Kevin, he said: 'Now, the thing is, Kevin, that we're the' – he paused proudly – 'Time Bandits.'

'You *are*?' asked Kevin with wide eyes. Then thinking, he added, 'What are the Time Bandits?'

'A gang of desperate, international – no, intergalactic –

robbers who know no boundaries of time or space. What we do is pull a job in one age – say Ancient Assyria – then before you can say knife we pop down a convenient time-hole and we're in the twenty-first century in Bulgaria,' said Randall, puffing up his chest. 'Now, what we've got to do is sneak into Castiglione without the French soldiers seeing us.'

'But why?' Kevin asked.

'That's where Napoleon is, isn't it?'

'Well, yes.'

'Don't you want to see Napoleon?' Randall asked, winking at the other dwarves.

'Yes, of course,' said Kevin, 'but do you really think we can?'

'No problem,' said Randall cockily. 'Now what we need is a sure-fire way to get safely into town.'

'Oh, great,' said Kevin enthusiastically.

'Shhh,' Randall said. 'I'm thinking.'

Just then, a large farm cart rumbled across the bridge and came to a halt on the side of the road just above them. In it an old man was noisily proclaiming that he was on his death bed, and several of his womenfolk were weeping lustily.

'Dammit,' shouted Randall, shaking his fist at the refugees, 'can't you flee a bit more quietly? I'm trying to concentrate. Now. . .'

'You mind your manners, young man,' shouted the old farmer. 'I'm dying.'

'Well, die a bit more quietly, won't you?' Randall said. 'I can't hear myself think.'

'Water,' cried the old man, ignoring Randall, 'I must have water.' Two of his sons hoisted him out of the wagon and carried him down to the river, followed by the wailing women of the family.

Strutter, looking around, noticed the untended wagon and nudged Randall in the ribs. 'I've got an idea,' he said. 'Quick!'

After a whispered consultation, the dwarves rushed up to the cart, threw all the farmer's belongings into the road, and began to knock the cart's wheels off with clubs. Then they heaved the wheel-less conveyance over the bridge and into the river.

Then, grabbing a few cooking utensils to use as paddles, the dwarves and Kevin rushed down to the river and jumped into their newly made raft. As they passed the old man at the side of the river trying to drink, Og handed him a cup from the cart.

'Thank you, very kind – ' began the old farmer, but then he recognized both the cup *and* the cart they were floating in. 'Here!' he shouted, helplessly as the dwarves, paddling and laughing, headed towards Castiglione. Kevin sat on the tailgate looking into the setting sun and thinking about meeting Napoleon.

—4—

INTO THE BURNING CITY

Under cover of darkness, Kevin and the Time Bandits cautiously edged up from the river into the ravaged city of Castiglione. The scene was one of desolation and ruin. Whole areas of the city were in flames, and the acrid smoke drove citizens into the hands of French soldiers who herded them aimlessly like cattle, looting as they went. Dead animals floated in the water, and the wounded lay in the streets, waiting vainly for attention and crying with pain. Not far away, the ragged sound of musketry confirmed that the shooting was not yet over.

'Shhh,' said Randall to the others, as the seven crept into Castiglione's ruined town square.

'But where are we going?' asked Kevin.

Just then, over the confusion of sounds came the high-pitched sound of a man laughing uncontrollably. It seemed to come from a small theatre just across the city square. 'Check it out,' commanded Randall, with a nod to Strutter.

Strutter melted into the shadows, and after a few nervous moments he was back. 'That's it,' he said to Randall. 'That's where he is.'

'Follow me,' said Randall.

At the back of the line, Kevin whispered to Strutter: 'What are we going to do?'

'Shhh,' said Strutter.

'A robbery,' said Fidgit helpfully.

'A robbery?' asked Kevin.

'Of course,' said Fidgit a bit indignantly. 'That's what international criminals do. We do robberies.'

'Shhh,' said Randall. 'Quiet at the back.'

Outside the little theatre, the seven stopped in a dark shadow and watched the guards marching up and down in front of the entrance.

'Who are you going to rob?' Kevin asked Randall in a whisper.

'Who else?' asked Randall. 'Napoleon.'

'Napoleon?' Kevin couldn't believe it.

'That's right,' said Randall complacently.

'But he's *Napoleon*.'

'And he's rich.'

'But. . .'

'Shhh!' said Randall, motioning the others to follow him.

Inside the little theatre was a very strange scene. All of the seats were empty except one, and that was occupied by a little man in an elaborate general's uniform with a hat square on his little round head. The general's right hand was stuck inside his tunic which was weighed down with medals. On the small stage, lighted by burning tapers, was an even smaller puppet stage, and in it was being performed a Punch and Judy show.

'Take that!' cried the tiny Punch, beating Judy with her own rolling-pin.

The one-man audience was rolling about in his seat with helpless laughter, but he seemed to be the only happy person in the theatre. At the back, under the balcony, Napoleon's generals, all tall, rather gaunt figures, huddled and talked morosely among themselves as their leader cheered and laughed at the antics of the boisterous puppets. Beside the generals were the mayor and town elders of Castiglione, all bound in chains and all looking even sadder than the generals.

'More! More!' cried Napoleon, as the tiny puppets took their bows and the small red and yellow curtain fell. Just then, one of his generals moved to his side and leaned down diplomatically.

'Monsieur Commander . . . the Mayor of Castiglione and his Council would like very much to surrender now, if you please. . . .'

'Later, Lucien,' Napoleon said with a wave of his only visible hand. 'More, little fellows, more!' he cried to the vanished puppets.

'But sir,' insisted General Lucien, 'the surrender of Castiglione would be a marvellous feather in our cap . . . we would have the whole of Western Lombardy at our feet.'

'They are very anxious to surrender,' added General Neguy, another elongated officer of Napoleon's staff, as he joined his commander and Lucien. 'They have been waiting for more than eight hours.'

Napoleon looked up sourly at the towering generals on either side of him. 'Don't stand so close to me, Neguy,' he said. 'I've warned you about that. You on one side . . . 'im on the other – ' he gestured to Lucien. 'It's like standing at the bottom of a well.' The generals hastily retreated a few steps and tried not to look so tall.

'Just because you think I'm small,' Napoleon continued bitterly, 'you . . .'

'Oh, no!' insisted Neguy. 'You're not small, Commander . . . not small at all.'

'No, not by any means,' added Lucien. 'Five foot one is *not* small.'

'Five foot one *and* conqueror of Italy,' bragged Napoleon. 'Not bad, eh? Eh?'

'No, no,' said the generals together, 'very good indeed.'

'All right then,' said Napoleon, turning back to the silent stage. 'More!' he demanded, slapping his thigh with his left hand. 'I want more puppets!'

Backstage, the theatre manager was in a cold sweat. Behind the tiny puppet theatre, the puppeteer lay on the stage floor, bleeding from a bullet wound, the Punch and Judy puppets still on his hands.

'You must do more,' the theatre manager insisted. 'Can't you hear him?'

'I hear,' said the dying puppeteer, 'but . . .' On his right hand, Judy, with a handkerchief between her arms, tried to stop the flow of blood from the wound in his chest.

'Please!' implored the theatre manager. 'Please! You can't die now . . .'

In the stalls, Napoleon, still demanding more puppetry, shouted to his generals: 'When was the last time a man of five foot one took Milan . . . eh?'

Both generals answered dutifully: 'Oh, a very long time, sir, I'm sure.'

Up on the puppet stage, a blood-stained Punch appeared, and Napoleon brightened up. 'Great!' he shouted. 'Now, we'll . . .'

But then Punch wavered and fell from sight, the puppeteer's legs suddenly stuck out below the stage, shook convulsively and were deadly still.

'What?' demanded Napoleon menacingly. 'No puppets? Where is the manager? I want the manager!'

Smiling desperately, the theatre manager edged on to the stage and squinted into the torchlight. 'Sir,' he cried with hopeless enthusiasm, 'we have many other acts. . .'

A volley of shots from a firing squad rang out.

'. . . For instance,' continued the manager, turning a queer shade of green, 'we have Zuzu and Benny.' He quickly motioned on to the stage a couple of tall clowns wearing huge floppy shoes and carrying three stilts. Zuzu and Benny were both about six and a half feet tall.

'No!' cried Napoleon, waving them off stage.

'Well, then,' said the manager, '. . . er . . . how about the Great Rumbozo?' A large man in a pink leotard tiptoed on stage looking very doubtful. 'He sings and lifts heavy things,' added the manager hopefully.

'Too tall,' called Napoleon scornfully. The Great

Rumbozo left the stage gratefully.

'No?' gulped the manager. 'Then . . . uh . . . how about . . . ah! This I think you will like. *Very* funny. The Three Idiots!' Peering backstage, he desperately summoned three very frightened men well over six foot tall wearing full beards and ballgowns. 'They are from Latvia,' he added, 'and they swallow brushes . . .'

'No! No! No!' shouted Napoleon angrily. 'They're all freaks. None of them under five foot two. What kind of a theatre are you running?'

'I'm sorry, sir, but . . .' Another volley of shots from a firing squad drowned his voice. Desperately, he made one last try: 'How about Mademoiselle Patsy, the female baritone . . .'

'No!' cried Napoleon. 'More of the funny show . . . with the little puppets hitting each other . . . that's what I like . . . little things . . . hitting each other!'

'But sir,' cried the theatre manager desperately, 'we can't possibly. Sadly, the puppeteer is . . .' Just then, he felt a sharp tug on the tail of his frock-coat and looked down to see Randall, just off stage, looking up at him and beckoning. 'Just a second, sir,' the manager said to his audience, 'I'll see what I can arrange.' He left the stage like a man going to be hanged.

'Good! Good!' shouted Napoleon, waving away his over-tall generals.

In a few moments, the curtain of the main stage went up, and there was a tatty fanfare from the terrified orchestra in the pit. The puppet theatre was gone, and Kevin, Randall and the other dwarves were all on stage in a bizarre selection of costumes. Awkwardly, they began to dance, bumping into each other, falling down, getting up and falling down all over again. Og stepped on Wally's hand and got punched in the nose. He retaliated by pulling Wally's hat down over his eyes and striking out at anybody he could reach. All the while they were singing horribly out of tune, 'Me and My Shadow'. Kevin, not knowing what else to do, jumped up and down and tripped over his own feet.

Backstage the manager, seeing Napoleon sitting perfectly still with a face of stone, rang down the curtain on the heap of tumbled dwarves and pulled a pistol from his pocket. With despairing eyes he placed the pistol to his head and pulled back the hammer with his thumb.

'Well?' asked Randall, struggling to get to his feet. 'What do you think?'

The manager was about to answer by releasing the hammer when suddenly he heard enormous applause and shouts of delight from Napoleon. As he lowered the pistol in amazement, Napoleon was suddenly backstage, followed by his bewildered generals.

Napoleon was shaking Kevin's hand and exclaiming: 'You stick with these guys, young man, and you'll have a great future.' He turned to the dwarves: 'You know, you are the best thing that has happened to me in this whole campaign. I came down here to conquer Italy because I thought they were all small, you know. I heard they were really tiny guys, but . . .'

General Lucien plucked at his commander's sleeve. 'Really, sir, we have important matters to . . .'

'Shut up!' exploded Napoleon. 'Don't tell me my business. You're fired, you hear . . . you, Lucien; and all of the rest of you great streaks of misery.'

'But sir . . .' began General Neguy.

'No!' insisted Napoleon. 'From right now I have *new* generals.'

In a very short while Kevin and the dwarves, wrapped in the enormous uniforms of Napoleon's general staff, were all sitting around a long banquet table, while the owners of the uniforms shivered out in the town square in their long underwear. At the head of the table, Napoleon, his only visible hand wrapped around a bottle of brandy, rambled on to his new general staff.

'Alexander the Great,' Napoleon recounted, 'five foot

tall exactly. Isn't that incredible? The man whose empire stretched from India to Hungary, one inch shorter than me! Oliver Cromwell . . . the only man with any guts in British history . . . not a big man . . . not a big man at all.' He took another generous swig of the brandy. 'Isn't that something?'

Kevin, nearly lost in General Neguy's Prussian-blue jacket with its heavy gold epaulettes, nodded sleepily, not knowing what to say. Randall and the other dwarves, similarly dressed, were too busy gawking at the mountain of plunder – gold, silver, precious stones, priceless works of art – piled up behind Napoleon to do more than wave agreement with gestures of their invisible hands in the long uniform sleeves.

'Louis XIV . . .' continued Napoleon, his voice even more slurred '. . . five foot three; Henry of Navarre, called Henry the Great, five foot two and a half; Charlemagne, a dumpy little five footer, squat little chap . . .'

Secretly, Randall studied the ancient map below the table. Pointing to a spot on it, he nudged Strutter and pointed towards the window leading out on the city square. Strutter nodded and slipped away from the table into the shadows as Napoleon droned on:

'Charles Martel, five foot three; Saladin, five foot one, same as me; Attila the Hun, only half an inch taller with his shoes on . . .'

Kevin looked from Napoleon to Randall to Strutter, wondering what on earth was happening.

'. . . Voltaire, only five foot two; Cyrano de Bergerac, five foot three and a half,' Napoleon continued, his head ever nearer the table, 'Tamburlaine the Great, four foot nine inches . . . and . . . three . . . quarters . . .' With a sigh, Napoleon slumped forward, his head thumping on the table, and the bottle of brandy rolled the length of the table.

Wally made a grab for it, but Randall smacked his hand sharply. 'There's no time for that,' he said. 'Strutter is outside locating a time-hole, and we've got exactly two minutes to gather up all this' – he indicated Napoleon's priceless stolen treasure – 'and get down the hole. At exactly midnight it disappears, so let's move!'

Ripping a priceless tapestry from the wall, they all began to fill it with the fabulous treasure, while Napoleon snored open-mouthed on the table, his short beaky nose in a pool of brandy. Even as he helped to stow away their loot, Kevin couldn't help feeling sorry for the famous little general.

Outside on the square, Strutter shouted: 'Atten-shun!' and all the soldiers – and the generals in their long underwear – froze where they stood while he searched desperately for the time-hole Randall had told him to find. Suddenly, he thought he'd found it, and with a glance at the town clock just reaching one minute to midnight, he rolled an unexploded cannonball towards where it ought to be. The cannonball disappeared instantly. Smiling, Strutter put two fingers in his mouth and gave a shrill whistle.

Inside the banquet hall, Randall heard the whistle, threw one more ruby-encrusted gold cup into the tapestry and shouted: 'That's it! Let's go!' As the others tugged the bulging tapestry towards the door, Og turned towards the sleeping Napoleon. Carefully, he removed the general's rings from his visible hand and then pulled Napoleon's other hand from his tunic. In the candlelight the hidden hand, made of solid gold, glittered and shone. Unscrewing it, Og dropped the precious hand into the collection of swag as it passed him. Kevin took one last regretful look at his fallen hero.

Outside on the square, Randall and the gang burst from the town hall like six lightning bolts, the bulky tapestry full of loot bumping behind them. They spotted Strutter across the square waving and headed in his direction.

As they passed the stiffly posed and freezing generals, Marshal Neguy glanced out of the corner of his eye and knew immediately what was going on. 'Thieves!' he cried. 'Robbers! After them!' Suddenly the French soldiers and the generals, dressed only in their long underwear with their long swords, dangling awkwardly by their sides, getting hopelessly in their way, were chasing after Kevin and the dwarves.

'Hurry!' cried Randall. 'Hurry!'

As the minute hand of the clock in the tower lurched towards midnight, the gang – only a few feet ahead of the pursuing soldiers – made a mad dive for the time-hole and disappeared just as the first stroke of the clock was heard. The flying soldiers, finding themselves with no quarry, suddenly stopped stumbled over each other and fell in a growing heap while their generals stalked around shouting orders and waving their glistening swords.

—5—

NEXT STOP – NOTTINGHAM FOREST

Once again, Kevin and the dwarves – and their bulging bag of treasure – were tumbling through time and space, distorting, twisting, changing shape and then re-forming as they fell through an endless, lightless, soundless void.

Soft spring sunlight dappled on the roof of a dusty coach and four as it hurried and jolted through the thick, tangled forests of Nottinghamshire. The driver, a burly man in a rough leather jerkin, flailed at the horses and urged them on towards the channel port of Dover.

Inside the coach, an ardent youth clad in a rich silk tunic clasped the hands of his heavily cloaked lady and sighed: 'Pansy!'

'Vincent!' responded his lady love.

'Pansy!'

'Vincent!'

'Pan–'

Suddenly, the roof of the coach burst open as, out of the sky, Kevin, the dwarves and their precious plunder crashed down on top of the lovers in a cascade of gold, jewels and precious artifacts. The coachman reined furiously; the horses bolted, and the coach tilted dangerously and then tipped over with a crash spreading Time Bandits, lovers and loot all over the lush grass.

'Robbers!' cried Vincent, picking Lady Pansy and a bulging bag of gold coins from the wreckage and fleeing into the forest.

'We did it!' said Wally, looking around as if he could

hardly believe it.

'Of course we did it,' said Randall. 'I told you, stick with me and you can't go wrong.'

'Sometimes I almost believe you, Randall,' said Wally, ducking a priceless jewelled chalice that Randall threw at him.

'Where are we?' asked Fidgit.

'Yeah,' said Og. 'Where . . . and when?'

'Well,' said Randall, 'it's pretty obvious to me that . . .' He turned the map to several different angles and studied, clearly bluffing. 'Er . . .'

Kevin, in wonder, almost to himself, murmured, 'We're in the Middle Ages.'

The others all chorused their amazement.

'Sure,' said Randall, gaining confidence, 'the Middle Ages, I could have told you that. Five hundred years before the man we just robbed was even born. Try that in a court of law!'

Wally prised the cork out of a bottle of Napoleonic wine. The dwarves cheered and cavorted under the big trees like madmen.

'Hey,' said Wally, taking a porcelain figure of the Goddess Ceres from Vermin, 'that's not meant to be eaten.'

'You never know until you've tried,' said Vermin.

'Are you always like this when you've done a raid?' Kevin asked Fidgit, watching the clowning dwarves in wonder.

'I don't know,' said Fidgit. 'This was our first one.'

'I thought you said you were international criminals,' said Kevin accusingly.

'We are *now*,' said Randall triumphantly. 'We sure are now.'

'That's right,' said Fidgit. 'Especially now that we've got Kevin.'

'Hang on! Hang on!' cautioned Randall. 'He's just a kid. Kevin's not one of us.'

'He knows an awful *lot*, Randall,' Fidgit said.

'And he's bigger than any of us,' added Wally.

'We can always use another pair of hands,' said Strutter.

Just then, Vermin appeared with a big wicker container. 'Hey, look at this,' he exclaimed happily, looking into it. 'Napoleon's packed lunch.' He tipped up the big hamper and a profusion of food, fruit, cakes and bottles poured out on to the grass. As the others descended on the goodies, Randall took Kevin to one side.

'Well, Kevin,' he said, 'do you *want* to join us?'

'Can we really go anywhere . . . into any age?'

'You name it,' Randall said, tapping the map meaningfully. 'If it's down here. . .'

'But how?' Kevin asked.

'This map used to belong to the Supreme Being, that's all,' said Randall hotly.

'You mean, you stole it?'

'No! Well, yes . . . I mean, sort of . . . you see, He was our employer. We worked for Him.'

'Worked for Him doing what?' asked Kevin.

'Creating the world, that's all,' said Randall, gesturing widely. 'He did the big stuff – good and evil, night and day, men and women, that sort of thing. And *we* did the trees.'

Kevin looked around them at the sylvan glade. He was impressed. 'They look pretty good to me.'

'They are!' insisted Randall. 'But did we get a thimbleful of credit?'

'No, sir!' called Wally, who was trying on a gold and diamond circlet which had once belonged to Eleanor of Aquitaine.

'Oh, no,' Randall went on, 'all we got was the sack for creating the Pink Bunkadoo.'

'The pink what?' asked Kevin.

'Bunkadoo,' said Wally. 'Lovely tree. Og designed it. Six hundred feet high, bright pink and smelt awful.' He held his nose.

'So,' Randall continued, 'to punish us, the Supreme being sent us down to the repairs department. Between you and me, Kevin, being created so quickly and all, the universe is a bit of a botched job. We discovered – ' He lowered his voice confidentially '– that there are *holes* in it.'

'Holes?' asked Kevin.

'Yes. Holes in time and space. And we've got a map showing every one. We thought – *I* thought – instead of *repairing* the holes, why not use them? Why not use this map – the only one in the universe – to get stinking rich!'

'Yeah,' said Strutter, 'stinking rich!' Plucking an earthenware jar of wine from the wreckage, he broke the wax seal and began to pour the wine out into precious chalices, silver goblets and even a ruby-encrusted helmet.

Raising high their vessels of wine, the dwarves all cried: 'Here's to stinking rich!

'And Kevin!' shouted Fidgit.

'Yeah,' said Og, getting confused, 'stinking Kevin!'

Just then, Kevin remembered the instant camera which he still carried in his school satchel. 'Hold it!' he cried. 'I'll take your photo.'

The dwarves all bunched together wearing broad grins as Kevin squinted through the view finder. 'Smile!' he called. Randall proudly unrolled the map to make sure that it got into the photograph.

'Got it!' said Kevin, pushing the button. 'And now. . .'

But just then a piercing shriek shattered the calm of the forest. 'Help! Robbers!' cried a woman's frightened voice.

'We sure are,' said Og.

'Save us!' screamed the voice, joined by another, deeper one.

'Someone's in trouble,' Randall said. 'Come on!' the gang grabbed up their bundle of swag and hurried in the direction of the cries for help. Less than a hundred yards away, in a dark dank part of the woods, they saw Vincent and Pansy, the young couple from the coach, tied to a tree while a group of filthy, ragged, evil-looking men were stripping them of their money, jewellery, Vincent's fine silk tunic and their tickets to France.

'Stop!' whispered Randall, pulling Kevin behind a thick ash. The other dwarves gathered behind them.

'But,' Kevin protested, 'aren't we going to help –'

'Shhh,' said Randall. 'Watch and learn something. These are *our* kind of people.'

'Yeah, they're not bad, are they?' said Wally, and they all gazed at the robbers admiringly.

Soon the gang had all the couple's valuables, and with much evil chuckling and spitting at Vincent's feet, they slipped into the undergrowth.

'Come on!' Randall said, leading his little band from their hiding place as Pansy cried one last, desperate: 'Help!'

When she spotted the Time Bandits, her hopes rose. 'At last! Someone's coming!'

But instead of stopping, the dwarves rushed past the couple tied to the tree, trying to keep up with the robbers.

'But aren't we . . .' Kevin began.

'Keep going,' said Randall. 'We'll lose them!'

'Help! I say!' Pansy called vainly. 'My fiancé and I would care for some help.' But soon Kevin and the dwarves had disappeared into the woods.

'Oh, Vincent,' cried Pansy.

'Oh, Pansy,' said Vincent. And it started to pour with rain.

Further on in the woods, Randall and the others were stealthily stalking the robbers who had just entered a crude camp of rough tents made of animal skins and bark. Campfires belched smoke, and the smell of searing meat hung in the heavy air. Laughter and shouting could be heard from many gruff and hearty voices.

'That's it,' said Randall, 'their headquarters. Right, lads, we're going in.'

'In *there*?' said Kevin incredulously.

'Sure. They're robbers like us, aren't they? They could give us a few tips as to where the action is around here.'

'I don't like it,' said Fidgit. 'Let's go home.'

'Don't be so wet,' said Randall scornfully. 'Just follow me. I know what I'm doo–!'

With the very first step the gang had taken, each had stepped into a carefully hidden snare, and within an instant they were all whisked into the air and left dangling upside down from a tree like so many Christmas presents. As they hung there, a group of scarred and evil-looking men stepped out of a bush. They approached the dangling Time Bandits with razor-sharp knives in hand.

'You just leave this to me, lads,' said Randall, trying to regain some of his swagger.

'What'll we do?' quavered Wally.

'Just watch me,' said Randall. As the leading robber approached with a wicked smirk on his face, Randall demanded loudly: 'What do you want, you tatty old ratbag?'

'Your business . . . Gobface?' spat the robber.

'Robbers.'

'*Villainous* robbers?' demanded the rogue.

'The worst,' said Randall, looking upside down into the robber's black-smeared, horrible face.

'Stop at nothing?'

'Nothing,' growled Randall.

'Steal the cup from a beggar's hands?'

'Of course,' Randall boasted.

'Teeth from blind old ladies?'

'Rather!' exclaimed Randall.

'Toys from babies?' the inquisitor demanded, his nose less than a millimetre from Randall's.

'*And* the babies,' said Randall, looking sinister.

The robber leader thought long and hard, scratching his grizzled chin with a wicked dagger. Then, with a look at the other thieves, he finally said: 'Right! Cut them down!'

The robbers cut the vine snares, letting the Time Bandits down with a thump. As they picked themselves up, the robber leader added: 'You *looked* a horrible lot, but we can't be too careful.'

'Thanks, brother,' said Randall.

'Except *that* one,' exclaimed another robber, pointing at Kevin. 'He looks a bit *honest* to me.' He raised a jagged hunting knife menacingly.

'*Is* he?' demanded the leader.

'Honest?' said Randall. '*Him*?' Oh, no . . . no . . .'

'He looks a bit clean, too,' said another robber with scummy green teeth, and very few of them.

'Oh, no,' said Fidget, covering up desperately. 'That's a skin complaint. He can't help it. Watch out *you* don't catch it.'

'I don't know,' said the robber, grabbing Kevin by his collar. 'I think this happy little face ought to look a little more lived in, eh, boys? I mean, rogues should look like rogues. Let's just . . .'

The robber reached for his sheathed dagger, but Wally deftly got there first, whisked the dagger from the sheath and secretly slipped it to Kevin.

As the robber whirled around angrily, Kevin held up the dagger and asked innocently: 'Is this yours, sir?'

'You're a real little thief,' exclaimed the robber admiringly, and everybody laughed.

'Come on,' said the robbers' chief, 'gather up all that beautiful loot and come with us. You've got to meet our leader.'

'Leader?' asked Randall. 'You mean you're not. . .'

'The leader?' said the robber. 'No, not me. I'm just one of the gang. You haven't seen anything until you've seen our leader.'

'Our leader! Our leader!' chorused the rest of the robbers.

'Well, I don't know,' said Randall nervously.

'Don't worry,' said the robber sinisterly. 'He'll like *you*. When he sees what you've stolen, you'll be his regular blue-eyed boys. Come on!'

—6—

MR HOOD, I PRESUME

The robbers led Kevin and the band of doubtful and nervous dwarves into their camp, a motley collection of tents stitched together from animal skins, and a huge campfire with a deer on a spit roasting over it. Grease from the cooking meat dripped into the fire, raising clouds of thick smoke. All around, tough-looking characters lounged against trees drinking thirstily from jugs. At a rough table of planks, two giant men in deer-skin jerkins arm-wrestled. With an oath, one of them triumphed, and in a sporting gesture held his opponent's arm high in the air. Unfortunately his opponent was no longer attached to it.

'Come on, you lot!' the winner crowed. 'I like a challenge!'

When the forest robbers saw Kevin and the dwarves, they crowded around with menacing curiosity. 'Who's this, then?' voices cried. 'What do *they* want?'

'Back off, boys,' said their guide. 'You just wait here,' he told Randall and the others. 'I'll go tell the boss you're here.' He disappeared into a nearby tent.

At this, the ferocious robbers fell back, muttering, 'The boss! The boss!' and Kevin couldn't help wondering what he'd be like.

In a few moments, the robber reappeared, and with him was a tall, lean man immaculately clad in a Lincoln-green outfit of finely tanned deerskin. He had a kind and gentle face and leaned slightly forward from the waist with his hands clasped low behind his back. He looked and spoke rather like a minor member of the royal family.

Extending a big hand to Randall, he said in a soft, well-modulated voice: 'Hello, I'm Hood . . .'

Kevin couldn't control his excitement. 'It's Robin Hood,' he whispered, nudging Fidgit in the ribs.

'Who?' said Fidgit. The other dwarves took this information very lightly until the robber who had guided them turned on them like a sergeant-major and screamed:

'Say 'Good morning', you scum!'

'Good morning you scum!' chorused the dwarves nervously in a ragged chorus.

'Good morning,' said Robin Hood pleasantly. 'You're all robbers then?'

'The best, Mr Hood,' said Randall.

'Jolly good,' said Hood, adding to Og, who looked at him in speechless wonder, 'You're a robber, too, are you?' When Og just goggled at him, Hood said, 'Jolly good,' and moved on to Wally.

'And do you enjoy robbing, then?' he asked him.

'It helps to pay the rent, sir,' said Wally.

'Ha, ha,' laughed Hood, 'that's jolly good, that is. Ha! Ha!'

Stepping up to Strutter, Hood extended his hand and asked: 'And you're a robber, too, are you? And how long have you been robbing?'

'Four foot one,' said Strutter.

'Good lord,' exclaimed Hood. 'Jolly good. Four foot one?'

'Yes, sir,' said Strutter.

'Well, that *is* a long time, isn't it?' said the robbers' leader. 'Well, now, I hear you have made a pretty good haul.'

'See for yourself, sir,' said Randall. 'Strutter! Wally!' he snapped over his shoulder, and the two came forward, straining mightily with the loot. They opened the tapestry, and the treasures gleamed richly in the warm sunlight.

'Gosh! I say!' exclaimed Robin Hood, looking over the loot. 'Crikey! I mean, I've been robbing for years, and I've never seen anything like this! Crumbs! You acquired all this by yourselves?'

'Well, it was a good day, Mr Hood,' Randall said modestly.

'Jolly good day!' agreed Robin Hood.

'It *is* nice, isn't it?' said Randall proudly.

'Rather!' said Hood. 'I mean, what can I say? Thank you, thank you, thank you all very much indeed.'

'Don't mention it,' began Randall. 'It's just – what?'

'Well, I mean, it's frightfully kind of you. The poor are going to be absolutely thrilled. Have you met them at all?'

'Who?' asked Randall, puzzled.

'The poor,' said Hood.

'The poor?'

'Oh, you must meet them,' said Hood. 'I just know you'll like them. Charming people. Of course, they haven't got two pennies to rub together, but that's because they're poor – ha, ha, ha!' Robin Hood's number two stared meanly at the dwarves until they joined him in the general laughter at Mr Hood's joke.

'Marion,' Hood asked the most vicious-looking of his men, 'would you be so kind as to ask the poor to come in, please?'

'No problem,' said Marion, smiling cruelly at the dwarves.

'Thank you so much,' said Hood, turning back to the big pile of loot.

'Now, let's see . . .' he said, beginning to sort it out into little piles. 'That's good . . . that's nice . . . that's *very* nice. It will be so much help in our work.'

'Umm . . .' Randall began. 'Excuse me. . . ?'

'Yes?' asked Robin Hood. 'Did you want a receipt. . . ?'

'That's *ours*,' Randall complained. '*We* stole that.'

'Oh, I *know*,' said Hood, 'and, believe me, the poor will be terribly grateful.'

'Yes, especially with Christmas coming up, Robin,' said a giant bowman whose nose had apparently been bitten off.

'Look here,' insisted Randall. 'That belongs to us. . .'

But two heavyweight robbers blocked his way as Marion reappeared, leading a long line of ragged peasants. As they passed Robin Hood, he gave them each one item from the Time Bandits' swag. Randall groaned as Hood handed a pox-scarred old man a solid gold bust of the Emperor Tiberius.

'Say thank you,' growled Marion hitting the peasant on the head with a stout club.

'Uhhhnnn . . . thank you,' said the peasant, falling in a heap at Hood's feet.

'You're welcome,' said Hood blandly. Turning to the dwarves, he asked: 'Would you like to stay and help us in our work? There's *so* much to do. . .'

'Oh, *I*'d like to stay,' said Kevin. 'Please!'

'And who are you, little boy?' asked Robin Hood kindly.

But before Kevin could answer, Randall grabbed him by the arm and pulled him away. 'Come on,' he said with disgust, 'we're leaving.'

'But . . .' said Kevin, 'I wanted to. . .'

'Never mind,' said Randall, and the dwarves followed him away into the forest, sneaking little longing glances at the treasure they were leaving behind.

'Thank you!' Hood called, just as they were leaving the clearing. 'Thank you *so* much!'

'If he says "thank you" once again,' Randall said between gritted teeth, 'I'll go back and kill him.'

A little later, far from Robin Hood's camp, rain was falling and a bitter wind chilled the Time Bandits as they strung single-file through the forest. A fork of lightning cracked the darkening, wild, forbidding sky, and the once-sunny atmosphere was suddenly dangerous.

As they emerged into a glade, there were Vincent and

Pansy still lashed to the tree and now soaked to the skin, being robbed yet again. This time by a trio of ex-monks in dark, woollen cowls were robbing the couple of what little they had left.

Ignoring the wretched couple, Randall muttered: 'We are *not* a charity organization. We're *thieves*! The poor!' he spat.

'Excuse me!' cried Pansy sadly as they passed. 'Excuse me!'

'We could have at least stayed and talked to him,' said Kevin.

'Oh, I say . . .' said Vincent as one of the ex-monks removed his Moroccan leather shoes.

'Talk!' said Randall. 'He'd probably steal your words, too.'

'I'll never get a chance to meet Robin Hood again,' Kevin moaned. 'All my life I. . .'

'Yoo-hoo,' called Pansy. 'Any chance of a rescue?'

'Stop moaning,' said Randall. 'Hood's obviously a dangerous man, unbalanced if you ask me. Giving away what isn't even his!'

'Of course he gives it away,' said Kevin. I know that . . .'

'Oh, you know it all, you do!' said Randall in a rage.

'Leave him alone, Randall,' said Strutter.

'Can't we stop pretty soon?' asked Fidgit. 'I'm getting tired.'

'Well, he makes me sick,' said Randall, turning on the others. 'Anyone who's always right makes me sick.'

'That's why you get on so well with yourself, then,' said Wally.

'Watch it!' Randall warned him.

'Well, you *have* got us lost,' Strutter reminded him.

'We're *not* lost,' said Randall indignantly.

'Well, then,' asked Fidgit, 'where *are* we?'

'Well. . .'

'Give me that map, Randall,' said Strutter. 'I'm taking over.'

'You're not.'

'I *am*!' insisted Strutter.

'Give it to him, Randall,' said Fidgit.

'Keep out of this,' said Randall.

'Give it to *me*,' butted in Wally. '*I'm* taking over.'

'Leave off!' warned Randall.

'*I'm* taking over,' cried Fidgit.

'No, me,' they all cried in a jumble of words, 'I'm taking over,' and several sets of hands grabbed for the map. Punches were thrown and Fidgit got pushed into a little ice-cold stream.

'Now stop it,' said Kevin, trying to separate the brawling dwarves, but they were too busy fighting. He got pushed to the side and stood watching helplessly.

Suddenly the rain slackened, and a cold wind struck up, making Kevin hug himself for warmth. The wind increased, and Kevin had an uneasy feeling that they were not alone. He didn't know it, but someone else was watching the angry dwarves as they fought among themselves. Kevin thought that he heard faint, distant, but menacing laughter.

—7—

A FEELING OF EVIL

'So these are the sort of people the Supreme Being allows to steal his map, eh?'

The speaker, and owner of the eyes which Kevin had felt spying on the Time Bandits, was peering down into a dank and mysterious pool of water. In its depths he could see the entire scene: the dwarves fighting and scuffling among themselves in the vastness of Sherwood Forest, and Kevin, off to one side, helplessly watching and trying to keep warm.

The speaker was Evil. Arthur G. Evil, to give him his full name, wore a scaly, breastplate like a crab's shell and a flowing red cape. His eyes, set in a long, pale face, brimmed with hatred as he stared into the water. On the shoulders of his cloak, knuckled claws served as epaulettes, and his entire outfit had the glistening slimy sheen befitting a creature from the dark depths.

'Aren't they pitiful?' he laughed mirthlessly. The small group of stunted creatures gathered around him echoed his laughter fearfully, keeping a wary eye on their master for the smallest hint of displeasure.

The murky grotto in which he stood, illuminated only by the tormented souls of poor creatures he'd bribed to his service, was Evil's prison as well as his command-post for spreading – well, evil – throughout the known world and several others which ordinary mortals can't even dream of.

For as powerful as he was, Evil could not leave the grotto deep in the bowels of the Fortress of Ultimate

Darkness, and his only contact with the outside world was through the mysterious pool in which he now watched Kevin and the others with such hatred. His long-nailed hands sliced the air over the magic pool as if to skewer the images in its depths. The dark water roiled and bubbled, its surface clouding with Evil's hatred, but he couldn't reach the dwarves, and that knowledge tormented him.

Looking about at his minions, creatures he *could* reach, Evil laughed again, his eyes smouldering beneath a cap decorated with a genuine, slightly used, skull. 'Look at them,' he commanded, 'the stunted little proles. *I* wouldn't trust them to wipe their own noses.'

His eyes lighted on a particular helper, a queer sort of fellow, half demon, half robot. 'Eh, Baxi?'

'No . . . no, Sire,' cringed Baxi-Braxilia III, a monstrous, deformed, half-witted hanger-on, '*much* too difficult for them. Wiping their own noses, I mean. I think.' He made a sincere effort to disappear into his own, pointed shoe.

'Who said *you* could think?' demanded Evil, and his other helpers laughed like automatons. They all began to edge away from Baxi.

'What sort of so-called *Supreme Being*,' Evil went on, 'would allow silly prats like *them* to steal his precious map?' He raked his servants with a penetrating gaze. 'That doesn't sound very *supreme* to me. Such a Supreme Being must be a complete and utter twit, must he not?'

The others all just nodded nervously, realizing gratefully that no answer was required or even allowed. All except Baxi, that is. With wide-eyed innocence he replied, 'Well, you have to admit that he *did* create you, Evil One.'

'What did you say?' Evil spat the words like a witch's curse, and all of the other minions sank back into the shadows of the grotto, leaving Baxi in the spotlight of their master's wrath.

'Well, your Awfulness,' Baxi stammered, 'I mean, he couldn't be such a *complete* twit, O Wicked One, if he created you in all your badness and . . .'

The world would never know how Baxi might have tried to get out of *that* one because Evil swivelled suddenly, raised a hand and pointed it. There was a sharp crack, a puff of smoke, and all at once Baxi was a small, smouldering pile of an unidentifiable substance.

'Don't *ever* say that," Evil commanded. 'No one *created* me! I am Evil, and evil existed long before good. I made *myself,* and I cannot ever be "unmade". I am all-powerful!'

His toadies, all except the late Baxi, applauded dutifully, and one of them, who was called Cartwright and looked a lot like an evil, warped, stunted gnome, only not so attractive, dared to go on:

'But why, your Nastyhood,' asked Cartwright, 'that being the case, are you unable to escape from this grotto deep in the bowels of the Fortress of Ultimate Darkness?'

Evil whirled to his left this time, extended his fatal finger, and Cartwright too disappeared in a small explosion, leaving only the smell of rotten eggs behind him.

'Good question,' admitted Evil. 'Why *do* I let the Supreme Being keep me here in the Fortress of Ultimate Darkness?'

'Well,' said Robert, a *very* trusted helper with absolutely no neck and very little forehead, cringing to make himself smaller, 'I suppose it's because. . .'

'Shut up!' snapped Evil. 'I'm going to answer that question myself.'

'Oh, of course,' grovelled Robert, glad to still be around even such a temperamental employer as Evil.

'I allow him to keep me here,' Evil continued, 'because – well, because I feel like it, that's why.' He looked about him closely for the faintest show of doubt, but nobody even breathed. 'If I really wanted to get out, I mean *really*, I could do it like *that*.' He snapped his long fingers like gunshots.

'Clever,' admired Robert. 'Very clever.'

'I am only waiting to get my hands on the map,' Evil declared, 'then I shall be able to escape from here and then the world will be a very different place, because I shall have understanding!' he screamed.

'Understanding of what, O Essence of Nauseousness?'

'Of digital watches. And then of video cassette recorders, and then heated toilet seats. And when I understand all of that, I shall understand computers. And when I understand computers, *I* shall be the Supreme Being. I . . . *Evil*.' He looked around sternly. 'What? No applause?'

Evil's followers applauded lustily, even risking a few cheers and a piercing whistle or two.

At that point one of his flunkies, who was not so much a creature as a vague, unpleasant shape, scuttled to Evil's side.

'Sir . . . sir . . .' said the shape, who was called Benson.

'. . . The Supreme Being is not interested in technology,' Evil went on, ignoring the interruption. 'He knows nothing of the potential of the microchip or the silicon revolution. Oh, no, he's obsessed with making the grass grow and getting the colours in rainbows right. He . . .'

'Sir . . .' Benson insisted. 'Sir . . .'

'I mean,' Evil ploughed on, 'look how he spends his time: forty-three separate species of parrot! I ask you! And *thirty-one* flavours of ice cream plus vanilla!'

'And slugs,' said Robert helpfully.

'Yes, slugs!' Evil crowed, almost choking with contempt. 'He *created* slugs. They can't speak. They can't hear. They can't operate machinery or salute. I mean, are we or are we not in the hands of a lunatic? Hmm?'

'Sir . . .' insisted Benson, daring to tug on the voluminous sleeve of his master. 'Look!'

'If *I* were creating a world,' Evil went on, still ignoring Benson, 'I wouldn't mess around with butterflies and daffodils. *I* would have started with lasers. And that would have been at eight a.m. on Day One!'

With a dramatic flourish, he spread his long arms wide, and a beam zapped accidentally from his fingers into the murky darkness behind him. There was a brief agonized cry.

'Sorry,' said Evil, half turning.

'I can't wait for the new technological dawn,' slavered Robert eagerly.

Becoming aware of Benson tugging on his sleeve, Evil looked down at him and snarled: 'Do you *want* to die?'

'Oh, yes, please!' Benson begged. 'But first, your Nastiness, I've seen the map. The map, sir. The Map!'

'What? Where?'

Jabbing excitedly towards the image of the squabbling dwarves in the pool, Benson gibbered: 'There, master, there! The little one has it.'

'Which little one?' demanded Evil, looking deep into the pool.

'This is our chance,' Benson said. 'This is what we've been waiting for.'

'It will set us free,' Robert added, then a bolt of fear shot across his imbecilic face. 'But not of you, master, not of you. Never!'

'Shut up,' Evil growled. 'If you are wrong, Benson,' he added, 'my revenge will be slow and unpleasant. I will turn you inside out over a very long period . . .'

'Oh, thank you, master,' Benson babbled. 'Thank you!'

'But now,' Evil said, 'we must bait the hook, see if they bite, and then pull them in.'

'Yes! Yes! Yes!' Benson and Robert chanted, though they didn't have a clue what he was talking about.

Evil drew himself up to his full height. 'Stand by,' he said, 'for mind control.' Folding his arms with an impressive flourish, he accidentally zapped himself. 'Ow!' Recovering, he said: 'Watch the little one called Og. He's our man.'

Meanwhile, back on the outskirts of Sherwood Forest, the dwarves had stopped fighting. They all looked worried and restless. Randall held the map and was studying it intently.

'Let's make up our minds and get out of here,' said Fidgit. 'I don't like it here.'

'What about Babylon?' Randall suggested, looking at the map.

'Who?' asked Wally.

'You ignorant heap,' said Randall scornfully. 'It was a city of legendary wealth in . . . er . . .'

'650 BC,' Kevin added helpfully.

Suddenly Og, who very seldom said anything at all, announced in a strange, disembodied voice, like a computer or a civil servant, 'I got a better idea.'

They all turned in wonder and stared at Og.

'Who said that?' Randall demanded.

'I got an idea forming,' Og continued, his mouth moving strangely as if it were being controlled by some distant force, 'in my head.'

'You haven't had an idea for thousands of years,' said Strutter.

Og went on as if he hadn't heard: 'There is a place where we could find the greatest thing a man could want . . . the goal of everybody's hopes and dreams.'

'What are you talking about?' Randall scoffed.

'The Most Fabulous Object in the World,' Og pronounced in his spooky voice.

'Hey, that sounds pretty good,' said Wally.

'Yeah,' said Strutter. The dwarves all began to look interested.

Except for Randall, that is. 'Hold on!' he demanded. 'We want hard cash, not some airy-fairy crock of gold nonsense.'

'It might be worth a try, Randall,' Strutter insisted.

In his grotto in the Fortress of Ultimate Darkness, Evil rubbed his hands with glee. 'They're hooked,' he gloated. 'Miserable, greedy little fish!'

But Kevin, noticing that Og's strange new voice seemed to have a powerful effect on the other dwarves, protested 'No,' he said. 'Why do we have to be after money all the time? Why can't we find a battle or a siege or something really interesting like that?'

In his lair, Evil frowned at the image in the pool. 'Who is *that*?' he demanded.

'I don't know, your Badness,' Benson said. 'I've never seen him before.'

'He is young, but stronger than the rest,' Evil said. 'His will defies me. But who *is* he?'

'I don't know,' repeated Benson. 'I. . .'

'I'm losing them,' Evil cried. 'I'm losing them!' He pressed his long taloned fingers on his forehead. 'There's something going on down there!'

In Sherwood Forest, as they argued Kevin and the dwarves were getting increasingly restless and frightened. The wind struck up again ominously, and in the distance, deep in the forest, there was just a hint of an unearthly glow. Randall was busy looking at the map. Wally looked up over his shoulder, and his eyes widened.

'Look, Randall,' he said urgently, pointing. 'Over there! We'd better. . .'

'Don't rush me,' Randall said, still busy with the map.

'The forest,' Wally insisted, 'it's on fire!'

'In this rain?' Randall said scornfully. 'Pudding head!' But he snatched a quick look over his shoulder, 'Oh, no!'

'What is it?' Kevin asked.

'It's Him!' said Randall.

'It's Him!' Fidgit agreed. The dwarves all backed in different directions, bumping into themselves, cowering from the growing brightness and trying to hide behind each other.

'He's found us!' Wally groaned.

'We're done for!' cried Fidgit.

'Quick! Quick!' Randall ordered, rolling up the map. 'We'll just make for the nearest time-hole . . . over there!'

The glow in the forest continued to come towards them. The wind howled. Trees and bushes were ripped up by the roots and flung through the air by an invisible force. The dwarves, in their eagerness to get away, tripped all over each other, allowing Kevin to sprint ahead towards the time-hole.

Behind them, the swirling glow changed into the shape of the Supreme Being. His voice rang out: 'Stop! I demand that you stop. Stop now before it is too late!'

But Randall, trying vainly to organize his gang, cried: 'Get to the hole. Any hole. Quick!'

Some way ahead, Kevin suddenly stopped in his tracks. Desperately he called back over his shoulder: 'There are *two* holes, Randall! Which one? Which *one*?'

'Just go!' screamed Fidgit, above the noise of the whirling wind and the Supreme Being's voice:

'Do not defy me!' Return the map!'

Kevin, taking one last despairing look, jumped through the nearest hole into the nothingness of the void. Just as he disappeared, Randall and the others lurched into sight with the Supreme Being close behind them, and plunged through the other time-hole.

'What the . . .' cried Evil in his grotto. 'We've lost them! We've lost them! Benson!'

—8—

THE MIGHTY WARRIOR

The next thing Kevin knew was that he was falling again – and all alone. Gone were the dank, wet, dripping trees of Sherwood Forest, and Kevin was descending through a clear, warm, azure-blue sky dominated by a sun which seemed to be three times the size of any he'd ever seen at home. Below was a high, barren plain the colour of sunburnt brick, fringed by distant blue mountains. And, in the middle of the plain, two giant figures were locked in deadly battle.

The larger warrior wore the half-rotted neck and head of a wide-horned bull over his own head, and wielded a great knotted club which he swung as lightly as if it were a toy. The smaller warrior, in a close-fitting Greek helmet which revealed only eyes as dark and bright as flint, brandished a short spear and fended off the crashing blows from the bull-head's club with a small round shield.

The battle was uneven as the bull-head shattered the hot, clear air with his great club, ever forcing the other warrior on to the defensive. But the smaller man fought back ferociously, keeping the bull-head at bay with his spear, and clouds of dust swirled about them as they raged back and forth.

Suddenly, a mighty swing of the bull-head's club caught the other warrior a glancing blow and threw him to the dusty, sun-baked earth. Dazed, his shield knocked away, and his short spear on the ground at his side, the warrior looked up at his pitiless foe. Closing in for the kill, the bull-head set his thick legs, and raised his great club to deal the crushing and killing blow. Feebly, the fallen warrior raised a leather-gauntleted arm in hopeless defence. The look in his eyes said that he knew he was all but dead.

But as the bull-head's club descended crushingly Kevin, still carrying his satchel, suddenly fell from the sky on to the armoured chest of the fallen warrior. In surprise, the bull-head delayed the killing blow for a split instant. That was long enough for the fallen warrior to snatch his spear and thrust it forwards and upwards desperately, striking between the ribs of his opponent just as the club began again to descend. With a shrill grunt, the bull-head let go of the club and grabbed for the piercing spear. Clutching its shaft, he fell dead on the dusty plain.

Automatically, Kevin had scrambled away from the descending club, and now he lay half dazed on the earth as the victor knelt over the dead bull-head. Getting to his hands and knees, Kevin began to crawl away, but turning from his vanquished foe, the warrior reached out and caught hold of the back of his jumper.

Pulling Kevin back towards him with strong arms, the warrior demanded. 'Where did *you* come from?'

Terrified, Kevin looked into the glinting eyes beneath the armoured cheekplates of his helmet, and could not speak a word. 'I . . . I . . .'

'Who sent you?' demanded the warrior. 'The Gods?'

Again Kevin was speechless.

'Zeus?' the warrior insisted. 'Athena? Apollo?'

But Kevin had no answers. He could only stare open-mouthed at the warrior in fear and awe.

Then the warrior released Kevin and, reaching up, removed his helmet, revealing a stern, sweat-streaked face and a short, curly beard. But when he smiled, the sterness was gone, and Kevin began to be less afraid. Still he could not speak.

'Well,' said the warrior in a milder tone, 'you're

certainly a chatty little fellow.' Bending down, the warrior drew out his dagger. Kevin shrank back in fear but the warrior only began to cut the bull's head from his dead foe.

Finding his tongue, Kevin blurted: 'I don't believe it!'

The warrior paused. 'You don't believe what?'

'The way you killed him. I can't believe it. . .'

The warrior's face clouded. 'Yes . . . but it has to be done. Sometimes.' He continued cutting away the bull's head.

'No, no,' Kevin insisted. 'I meant the *way* you did it. What a good *shot*! Right between the ribs.' He added with enthusiasm: 'I'll bet you've killed lots of people.'

The warrior smiled a bit distantly but did not answer. 'And you, little bloodthirsty warrior, the Gods must have given you some kind of a name.'

'Oh, yes . . . yes. It's Kevin.'

'Kevin?' The warrior repeated this strange name with bemusement. 'Well, do you want this, Kevin?' He held his helmet out to the boy.

'Oh, yes . . . yes, please,' said Kevin eagerly, holding out both hands to take it. But the warrior instead stepped forward and dropped the big leather-and-metal helmet over Kevin's head. 'It's yours,' he said.

'Mine?' said Kevin in amazement, his voice muffled inside the great helmet. 'I –'

'Don't you want it?'

'Oh, *yes*,' said Kevin. 'Yes, please. You mean I can really have it? To keep?'

'Yes,' said the warrior, 'but only on condition that you carry it back to the city for me.'

'No!' said Kevin, pulling off the hot, heavy helmet. 'I can't, really. I'd like to, but I have to – er – er wait here. You see,' he finished lamely, 'I'm with some friends.'

'Friends?' said the warrior, looking elaborately around them at the deserted, barren wastes. He smiled at Kevin, puzzled.

'I mean,' said Kevin, 'they'll be meeting me here soon.

If I lose them, I may never be able to get back. . .'

'Get back?' asked the warrior, still puzzled. 'Get back where?'

'I . . . I'm not sure.'

The warrior shook his head in wonder. Then, picking up the severed bull's head, he mounted a white stallion which had been waiting patiently throughout the battle. 'Well, take this, at least.' Unslinging a skin bag from his saddle, the warrior threw it to Kevin.

'What is it?' Kevin asked, catching the soft bag in both hands.

'Water. You'll need it.'

Taking the reins, the warrior swung the white horse around, and the horse began to canter away. But then, checking the horses, he looked back over his shoulder at Kevin. 'Whoever you are,' he said, 'Thanks.' Then, giving Kevin a last look, he spurred the horse into motion.

For a moment, Kevin stood clutching the water bag and looking around him at the vast expanse of burning nothingness. The warrior and his horse were just disappearing over a rise in the ground. Then, making a decision, he cried: 'No . . . no. I'd like to come with you, please!' He began to chase after the warrior's horse. 'Please . . . come back.'

The warrior reined in his horse, turned it back towards Kevin and with a smile leaned down and pulled the boy up on the saddle with him. Then, spurring the stallion into a gallop, they headed towards the city.

After they had galloped across the lifeless wastes for some time, a great walled city arose on the horizon, and the warrior steadily spurred on his horse in its direction. The city was a towering mud-brick edifice the colour of burnished gold in the dying rays of the sun, and Kevin thought that he had ever seen anything so magnificent.

'What is that city called?' he asked the warrior as they galloped ever nearer the massive walls, raising a torrent of dust in their wake.

'Mycenae,' said the warrior.

'But that's . . .' Kevin began, but his words were drowned in the blast of a mighty horn from high on top of the walls of the city. Before them, the great city gates were opened, releasing a torrent of people all shouting with joy. They were clad in tunics and robes that were familiar to Kevin from his books on Ancient Greece.

In a few moments, the warrior and Kevin were riding through the streets thronged by the cheering populace, who pelted the warrior with brilliant flowers and offered him presents from all sides. A path opened up through the mob almost as if by magic.

'You're a hero!' exclaimed Kevin, overcome by the welcome extended to the warrior.

'The warrior we killed was a great enemy of the city. Many here thought that they would never see me again – at least not alive.'

The welcome grew in size and fervour as they proceeded deeper into Mycenae. 'Where are we going?' Kevin asked, shouting over the clamour of the crowd.

'To the palace,' the warrior said. 'We must report to the king.'

'To the king?' Kevin said in wonder. 'We're going to see a king!'

'He owes us some thanks,' said the warrior, as they arrived at the gate of a luxurious palace. Handing Kevin down to a richly dressed servant, the warrior dismounted and was greeted by a party of officials. He bowed, and the officials bowed back. On a balcony above the gate stood a splendid throne, and beside it a slim, regal-looking woman wearing a chaplet of gold around her fine forehead. Kevin hung back as the officials began to lead the warrior up the marble stairs to the balcony, but the warrior beckoned for Kevin to follow him. When Kevin hesitated, the warrior took him by the arm and led him up the steps.

'Which one is the king?' Kevin asked.

'He hasn't arrived just yet,' said the warrior. 'Everyone has to wait for him.'

When they reached the balcony, the regal-looking woman and more officials greeted the warrior with formal smiles, and the multitude below fell silent. The warrior faced the crowd and raised the bull's head high over his own. Noticing that Kevin was staying back, he motioned for the boy to come to his side. 'You saved my life,' he told Kevin in a whisper. 'Remember?'

Then with a mighty fling, he threw the bull's head down into the cheering throng. 'The enemy is dead,' the warrior declaimed. 'Long live the freedom of the city.'

Great horns boomed out, and the crowd began chanting: 'Hail the king! Hail the king!'

'The king,' Kevin exclaimed, tugging on the warrior's sleeve. 'Is the king coming now?' He looked around but he could see no one else.

Then one of the officials stepped to the edge of the balcony and cried: 'Hail King Agamemnon!'

'Hail King Agamemnon,' the crowds in the street answered, and all eyes were directed at the warrior standing beside Kevin. Kevin looked up in wonder, and Agamemnon gave him a broad wink before returning his face to a suitably grave expression.

'Hail . . . Agamemnon!' the crowd repeated over and over again.

—9—

AT THE COURT OF AGAMEMNON

After a few days, it seemed to Kevin as though he'd always lived in Mycenae. King Agamemnon had put him into a fine suite of high, marble-walled rooms with servants and everything anyone could have desired. But really, the whole city was Kevin's domain just as much as it was Agamemnon's. When the king was busy, Kevin, dressed in the short tunic of a Mycenaean youth, roamed the city freely – the markets, the craftsmen's workshops, the great dyeworks with their long skeins of rainbow-coloured cloth, even the army's training grounds where the warriors learned to fight and kill.

But Kevin enjoyed most those times when Agamemnon allowed him to stay in the palace, in the great hall of state while the king was dispensing justice to his people. One day, in the great hall, while Agamemnon was attending to his kingly duties, Kevin was studying an ancient Thracian battle scene on a wall frieze.

'Gosh, Agamemnon,' he said, 'what a *brilliant* battle. Here's a man getting cut right in half!'

But Agamemnon sitting at his long table conferring with an adviser ignored Kevin. He was looking at a small scroll. 'They all four must die,' he pronounced. 'This day. If the queen has any objections, she can find me in the courts this afternoon.' The adviser bowed low and began to leave. At the door, the king stopped him. 'I still rule this city, Thersites. You may remind the queen of that fact.'

As the adviser bowed again and left, Agamemnon began to unroll another scroll. He looked troubled.

'I wish I'd been in the Trojan Wars,' Kevin said, 'and 'seen Priam and Hector. Just imagine all those javelins flying . . . and the swordfights!'

Agamemnon looked up from his work, smiling tolerantly. 'I *can*, believe me,' he said.

'Will you show me how to swordfight?' Kevin asked him. 'Please?'

'Come here,' said the king, 'and I'll show you something much more useful.'

When Kevin arrived at the long table, Agamemnon had overturned two of three empty goblets and held a round, red marble paperweight in his hand. 'See this?' he said, holding up the paperweight between thumb and forefinger. Then he put the paperweight down on the table and covered it with the third goblet. Swiftly, he moved the goblets around on the table with a fluid motion.

'Now,' he asked Kevin, 'where's the paperweight?'

'There' said Kevin, who'd been trying to keep track, pointing at the middle goblet.

The king turned it up, Nothing. Then another, with same result. Then he picked up the third goblet, and the paperweight wasn't there either. With a grin, Agamemnon reached out his empty hand and produced the small red ball from Kevin's ear.

'Kings aren't supposed to do things like that!' Kevin protested. 'It's not – it's not – kingly!'

Agamemnon just smiled and suggested that they go for a walk in the royal gardens. As they walked among the lush fruit trees and vines tended by legions of gardeners, Kevin doggedly tried to sort out his confusion.

'But I thought,' he said, 'that King Agamemnon was always fighting the enemy, that he was a *warrior* king. . .'

The king's face became sombre. 'Well, yes,' he agreed, 'but in between, when you're not fighting, that's the good time. That's when you have time to learn things . . . like

Kevin at home:
ːe adventure begins

The gang and the ːap: a celebration ːrtrait

△ 1

2 ▽

△ 3

4 ▽

3 **Napoleon and the Time Bandits:** making some military changes

4 **Major General Strutter:** leading the retreat

5 **Vincent and Pansy:** so much to worry about

6 **Sherwood Forest:** Robin Hood takes from the rich

5

6 ▽

7 △

7 **Ancient Greece:** Agamemnon and the bull-headed warrior fight

8 **Agamemnon's palace:** the King tests Kevin

9 **Aboard the *Titanic*:** Kevin won't listen any more

8

9 ▽

△ 10

11 ▽

10 **Mr and Mrs Ogre:** catching some strange fish

11 **The giant's hat:** the highest sea voyage ever known

Evil's jailhouse:
: gang hang

Og and Kevin:
ıfounded and
rounded

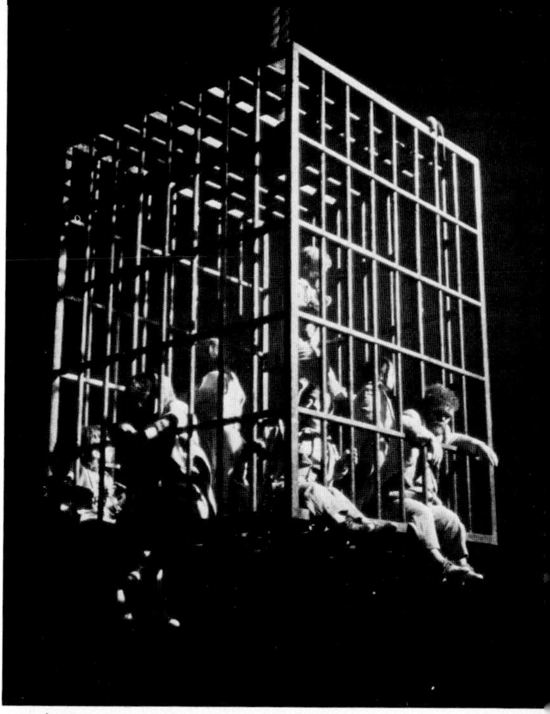

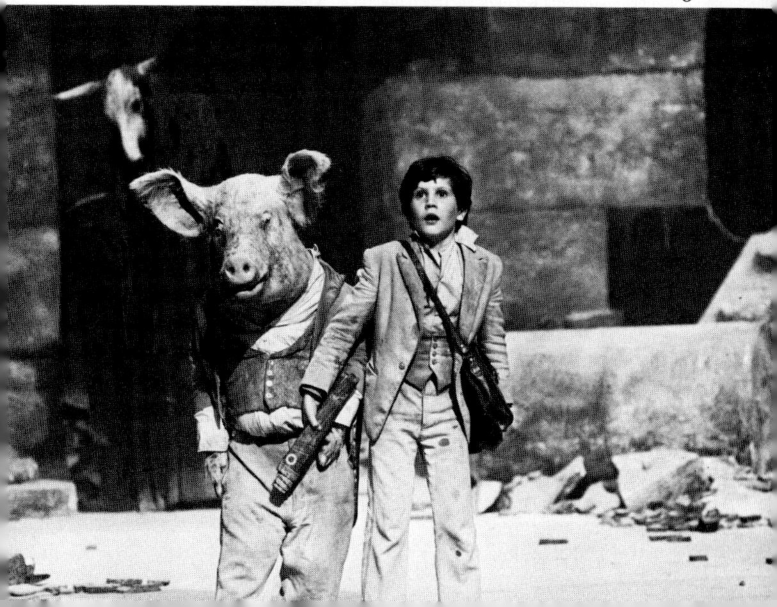

14 **The Supreme Being and Randall:** the map is returned . . . to its rightful owner

14

how to use one of these.' He reached down and pulled a knife from its sheath. It was very simple but beautiful, with a keen edge. He handed it to Kevin.

'Now I'll be able to kill the Trojans,' Kevin cried, making a mock stab at a passing gardener.

'No,' the king cried, grabbing the knife and cutting his hand in the process. 'Don't ever do that . . . never in fun!' He noticed the blood on his hand and calmed down. 'There are better uses for knives.'

Agamemnon picked up an apple from a pallet, handed it to a guard, and indicated that the guard should throw the apple in the air. The guard did, and invisibly fast Agamemnon's blade whipped through the air, impaled the apple and embedded itself in the trunk of a tree. After a pause, the apple fell to the grass, neatly sliced in half.

'Brilliant!' said Kevin.

Agamemnon stepped over and picked up the two apple halves. 'Do you like apples?' he asked, throwing Kevin one half and eating the other himself. He then pulled his knife from the tree.

'Oh, yes,' said Kevin, apple juice dripping from his mouth.

The king handed Kevin the beautiful knife. 'Take it then, it's yours.'

Later that afternoon, Kevin was on one of the highest towers of the palace, waiting for Agamemnon to finish his day's work. He stood on a parapet, taking in the beauty of Mycenae as the setting sun cast long shadows over its crowded streets with their hurrying crowds and playing children. Kevin knew he'd never want to forget this scene, so he took the Polaroid camera from his satchel and quickly took a snap of Agamemnon and one of his officials outlined against the beauty of Mycenae.

When the adviser had been dismissed and Agamemnon joined him on the parapet, Kevin said: 'You know, I never want to go back . . . to leave all this.'

'Don't you want to see your friends again? Those people

you were waiting for in the desert?'

Kevin grimaced. 'No . . . no thanks!' He'd had quite enough of Randall and the squabbling dwarves.

'Don't you want to be in your own home?'

Kevin paused to think, but after a moment he said: 'No . . . I don't think so.'

'. . . To be with your own father . . . your own mother. . ?' Agamemnon continued.

Kevin had to think again, and while he did so he looked out over the city's splendour to the awesome plain, and beyond that the glittering blue sea. Then he looked back to Agamemnon. 'No,' he said solemly.

'Well, then . . .' said Agamemnon.

'I can stay?' exclaimed Kevin.

'No more questions,' said the king. 'But go to bed early tonight and sleep well. I may have a surprise for you tomorrow.'

'What sort of surprise?'

'Wait until tomorrow.'

Kevin and Agamemnon parted solemnly. Then, as the boy was leaving to go to his quarters, he stopped in the doorway and turned back. 'Agamemnon,' he said.

The king looked up from a scroll he'd started to read. 'Yes?'

'All this,' Kevin began, 'it won't all suddenly go away, will it?'

'I said, no more questions,' Agamemnon said gruffly, but he smiled.

Kevin smiled, too. He paused again to wave, and then reached behind his own ear and produced the red paper-weight with a grin of triumph.

'That's good!' laughed Agamemnon, catching the paperweight which Kevin threw to him.

The next morning, Kevin woke early after a sound night's sleep. Stretching lazily, he watched the orange fingers of the rising sun creeping along the white marble wall over his bed. From his window, he could see the morning sky just changing from grey to a billiant Mediterranean blue.

Looking back from the window, Kevin was suddenly filled with alarm. Towering over his bed were two tall priests in black robes and golden masks.

'What – what do you want?' Kevin demanded, but the priests merely bent over him, and one placed a blindfold over Kevin's eyes.

All was darkness then and silence, as Kevin was led blindfolded through seemingly endless corridors. The priests led him gently but firmly.

'What are you doing?' Kevin asked. 'Where are you taking me?'

But the chief priest would answer only: 'These are King Agamemnon's instructions.'

Kevin felt the cool breeze of early morning on his face as he was taken out into a courtyard. He was lifted off his feet. The blindfold was removed, and Kevin found himself mounted on a magnificent horse with beautiful gold wings rising from its breastplate. A rich robe was placed around Kevin's shoulders, and his head was covered with a head-dress of woven gold cloth. He had to hold on tightly as the horse began to canter. Without being directed, the horse carried Kevin through a doorway off the courtyard.

Inside, Kevin found that he had been carried into a vast hall where Agamemnon's entire court was assembled. In the centre, Agamemnon sat on his splendid throne with Clytemnestra, his queen, a bit further off with her attendants. Beside Agamemnon's throne was a smaller throne, and Kevin was seated on it with great ceremony. From all over the hall, attendants came and placed precious gifts at his feet. Then Agamemnon rose majestically and held up his hands for silence.

'I have decreed,' Agamemnon told his court, 'that this boy shall remain here with us in our city. Furthermore, hear you all now and let it be known abroad that he shall be from this day forward my own son – heir to the throne of Mycenae!' The nobles gasped and then began to applaud dutifully.

Kevin was still taking in this wondrous event when Agamemnon signalled, and an attendant handed him a small gold-leaf crown which he laid carefully on Kevin's head. Around the boy's waist, the king strapped a slim golden knife. Then, grasping Kevin by the arm, he presented him formally to the assembled nobles of Mycenae.

'Now,' Agamemnon proclaimed, 'let the banquet and revels begin.'

To the sound of a loud gong, a great roasted ox on a spit was brought in and placed before the royal thrones. A gigantic slave with a shaven head raised high a long sword and split the ox in two, releasing an avalanche of oranges, apples, pomegranates and other fruit from inside the big beast. The nobles applauded madly as a beautiful girl extended a peach to the king, only to have it suddenly turn into a dove and flutter to the high ceiling.

Kevin leaned towards Agamemnon: 'You *really* mean that I can stay here forever?'

The king nodded with a smile, but then he was suddenly serious. 'In return,' he told Kevin, 'you must promise to remember all that I have taught you. Choose your friends with care, and never. . .'

But Agamemnon's lecture was interrupted by a drum roll and a flourish of trumpets. The king turned with a smile. 'Now,' he told Kevin, 'enjoy yourself.'

The heads of the assembled court turned as a troupe of entertainers came into the hall. They were three squat figures in fantastic costumes of feathers and furs with false horse heads jutting from their middles as if they were mounted riders. Cavorting about the hall to drum and pipe music, the mounted grotesques suddenly split in the middle, each becoming two, one masked and the other wearing a horse's head. In all, there were now six tiny, capering figures. Kevin was suddenly struck by a terrible suspicion.

It was quickly confirmed. The six clowns crowded to the dais holding the thrones and began to dance around the royal party. One by one they lifted their masks so that only Kevin could see their faces. They were none other than Randall, Strutter, Og, Fidgit, Wally and Vermin. Kevin was horrified.

They all winked knowingly at Kevin.

'Good work, Kevin,' Randall said. '*Very* good work.'

'Sorry we took so long to find you,' whispered Fidgit.

'Go away!' whispered Kevin, and he resisted as they began to try to lift him from his throne. He clung to it, but the dwarves insisted. Kevin looked to Agamemnon for help, but the king encouraged him to join in the fun.

'But Agamemnon . . .' Kevin cried in vain.

As Strutter and Wally nearly carried Kevin to a small platform in the middle of the hall, the other dwarves began capering around the hall, gathering up all the riches they could find, even taking pieces of jewellery from the delighted audience. Randall busily gathered up all the priceless gifts Kevin had been given on his crowning and put them on the growing pile on the platform. The assembled nobles began to pelt the dwarves with even more jewellery in anticipation of the fine trick they were hoping to see.

'We make a good team, eh, Kevin?' Strutter whispered. 'You set it up, and we come in just at the right time.'

'No!' said Kevin. 'Please!'

'What a haul!' gloated Wally.

Soon all the dwarves were on the platform with their rich booty, and Randall, consulting his watch, was counting down: 'Nine – eight – seven . . .'

Reaching down, the dwarves began to pull a wall of brightly coloured cloth up and around themselves, their loot and Kevin. 'Six – five – four – three. . .'

King Agamemnon and the others held their breath expectantly as the wall of cloth rose, completely obscuring the entertainers and Kevin.

'Two – one – blast-off!'

Suddenly the cloth dropped, and the entertainers, Kevin and all the treasure had vanished. The nobles applauded wildly, but gradually Agamemnon's delighted smile began to turn to a worried frown.

—10—
RANDALL'S NEW PLAN

'Pansy!'

'Vincent!'

On the afterdeck of a vast luxury liner, two young people dressed in sports clothes of the year 1912 were gazing ardently into each other's eyes. They curiously resembled the young couple who were robbed in Sherwood Forest.

'Isn't it glorious?' Pansy sighed, looking out into the dark, mysterious North Atlantic.

'I love the ocean,' Vincent proclaimed. 'She's so – so. . .'

'Wet?' suggested Pansy.

'Yes! that's it,' said Vincent, 'so – so wet.'

'Oh, Vincent!'

'Oh, Pansy!'

'Oh, Vincent.'

'Oh, Pansy. At last we're alone. . .'

At that precise moment, with a rending rip of the fluttering canvas awning above, six dwarves, Kevin and all their Mycenaean treasure came tumbling down on top of Vincent and Pansy, and crashed to the deck.

'Where the devil are we?' demanded Wally.

'Get offa me,' shouted Randall.

'Save me, Vincent,' Pansy cried. 'Vincent!'

'Blast you. . .' At last Vincent emerged from the chaos of jumbled dwarves and ancient Greek treasures. In the process he'd lost his toupee and was revealed to be totally bald.

'Vincent!' screamed Pansy. 'Your hair! It's not on your head!' She fled from the afterdeck.

'*Give* me that,' said Vincent to Vermin, who was about to eat his hairpiece. 'Wait, Pansy,' he cried, running after her. 'I can explain. Wait, my love.'

Some time later, the liner was aglow with hundreds of lights reflected dimly in the swelling sea. Elegantly dressed couples promenaded on the decks while the strains of dance music floated out on the cold moonlit night. Waltzing couples were silhouetted through a ballroom window, and Kevin and the dwarves were sitting on a first-class deck.

Kevin slumped disconsolately, staring out to sea and thinking of Agamemnon, but behind him, smartly dressed in black evening wear, bristling with gold watches and diamond shirt-studs, hair smeared with pomade, the dwarves reclined in deckchairs having the time of their lives. All were puffing on thick Havana cigars, emptying champagne bottles and throwing them over the side into the ocean.

Vermin snapped his fingers at the waiter. 'Six plates of caviare, please,' he said. 'Oh,' he added, turning to the others, 'does anyone else want any?'

'Nah,' said Wally, 'I'll stick to the quail's eyeballs, thank you. Caviare makes me throw up.' Catching a disapproving glance from Randall, Wally added hastily: 'Sorry . . . sorry, Randall.'

Og burped loudly, and they all turned and stared at him. 'Sorry . . . sorry . . . everyone.'

'Cheer up, Kevin,' Randall called out to the miserable boy staring out to sea. Kevin was also wearing black evening dress, but he wore it sadly, without the dwarves' jaunty air. 'Kings aren't the only ones with money.'

'The money wasn't important,' said Kevin without looking around.

'And you know why, Kevin, don't you?' Randall added. 'Because that old Agamemnon was stuck in

Ancient Greece, and he didn't have anything to spend it on.'

'You make me sick!' said Kevin, turning even further away from the carousing dwarves.

'Oooh, listen to him,' mocked Randall. 'Kevin's too good for money.' He exchanged cynical looks with the others, swigged another glass of champagne and sauntered over to where Kevin sat miserably. Leaning over the rail beside Kevin, he said confidentially: 'I've got something to tell you, Kevin.'

'Go away!' said Kevin bitterly.

'It's about the map,' Randall insisted. 'Something important.'

'The map,' said Kevin angrily. 'I don't understand you, Randall. You have something like that map – something really brilliant, that gives you all this power – and you're just wasting it.'

'I don't call this wasting it,' Randall said indignantly, gesturing towards the liner, the champagne and all the luxury. 'I mean, this isn't bad, eh? Not bad at all. I mean, it beats working for a living.'

'Why couldn't you have left me where I was happy?' Kevin demanded.

Randall looked about him with exaggerated caution, then leaned close and spoke confidentially to Kevin. 'Because you're going to be a lot happier,' he said, his eyes alight with enthusiasm, 'when you hear what we've got planned.' He leaned even closer to the boy. 'I was having a good look at the map last night, Kev, and do you know what I found?'

Randall paused impressively, and when Kevin didn't speak, went on: 'I found out that Og was right . . . the Most Fabulous Object in the World . . . it *does* exist!'

Randall waited for Kevin to react, but the boy just shook his head wearily. After another quick look all around, Randall reached into his dinner-jacket and brought out the map, and then squatted down beside Kevin, pointing.

'Look,' he said excitedly, 'I've discovered it. Down here is the place we've been looking for. It's called the Time of Legends, but it's sort of outside of time as *we* know it. There are giants, wizards, all that sort of thing. And *besides* that, right in the middle of the Time of Legends is this place called the Fortress of Ultimate Darkness, and inside *that* is the Most Fabulous Object in the World. Just as Og told us.'

'The Time of Legends,' Kevin scoffed. 'It doesn't exist.'

'But it *does*,' Randall insisted, '*if* you believe in it. If you *really* believe in it. That's what makes it true. Og has had some sort of message, and *I* believe it. You can, too, Kevin, if you try. You've *got* to.'

'Oh, rubbish!' Kevin turned away dismissively.

Randall took a quick, sneaky look at the other dwarves who were singing loudly and whistling at passing debutantes, and huddled closer to Kevin. 'You know,' he said, 'you and me have a lot in common, Kevin. We like a risk and we like adventure. Well, this is *it*. This is the *ultimate* adventure. None of your namby-pamby *ordinary* time-holes here. This is the big one. We stake all, and we win everything.'

'I've just *lost* everything,' Kevin said, 'and all because of you lot.'

'All right,' Randall said soothingly, 'I know how you feel. But there's no hurry right now. Just think it through. And remember, Kevin, whatever you may think of me now, I *did* get you all this.' He gestured broadly at the luxury ship and then beckoned to a hovering waiter.

'Yes, sir?'

'More champagne,' Randall ordered.

'Of course, sir . . .' The waiter hurried briskly away, revealing a large sign: SS *Titanic*.

'And lots of ice,' Randall called after him. 'Lots of ice!'

At that very moment, the great ship, the "unsinkable" *Titanic*, rammed into an iceberg and ripped a three-hundred-foot gash in her side. The holds filled with water.

Steam gushed as the great engines were drowned, and the passengers from first class to steerage panicked as the luxury ship began slowly to sink. Gradually, as the crew struggled to free the lifeboats, the deck tipped to a 45-degree angle, and the Time Bandits, still puffing on cigars and clutching champagne glasses, slid right off the deck and disappeared into the cold Atlantic Ocean.

The next thing Kevin knew he was deep in icy, green water fighting for air, struggling for his life. Just as he was about to give up, he flailed out an arm and struck something solid. Clutching it desperately, Kevin pulled himself up and discovered he was clinging to a big plank with the name 'SS *Titanic*' painted on it. He was all alone. In the misty distance, the great liner was tilted on its stern about to plunge to the depths. Cries of "Abandon ship!" and "Save me!" echoed over the sea, and horns and hooters sounded mournfully over the scene of desolation.

Above all this, a single voice could be heard crying plaintively: 'Pansy! I can explain everything!'

Kevin clung to the plank and for once he felt he would not have minded having the dwarves around. He even missed Randall. It was hard to believe that he would never see them again. But all that was in sight was wreckage and, in the midst a few crowded lifeboats being frantically rowed away from the sinking ship. Kevin raised an arm to hail one of the lifeboats, but nobody saw him.

He was just wondering how long it would take to drown or perhaps even freeze to death when suddenly with a loud pop Fidgit appeared from the depths and clung spluttering to the long plank. Then one by one the rest of the dwarves, all soaked and bedraggled and cold and miserable pulled each other out of the sea and on to the plank.

Kevin had never been so glad to see the Time Bandits. Of course they immediately started arguing.

'I want to go home,' Fidgit cried, desperately trying to keep his grip on the plank. 'I can't stand it, Randall.

You'll get us all killed.'

'Shut up, Fidgit,' Randall said. '*I* didn't know we were going to run slap-bang into an iceberg. It didn't say on our tickets: "Get off before the iceberg".'

'I suppose it's silly,' Strutter said, 'asking where the rest of the loot is.'

'It's safe, Strutter, absolutely safe,' Randall yelled back. 'It's all locked up in a specially made strong-box.' He reached into a pocket of his soaked dinner jacket. 'See, here's the key . . . 017 . . and as soon as they raise the *Titanic,* I'll be the first one aboard to – Vermin! Stop eating this plank!'

Vermin reluctantly stopped nibbling on the spar on which their lives depended.

'Help! Help!' cried Fidgit forlornly, and Wally joined in, too.

Just then, an evil wind wafted over the shipwrecked Time Bandits, and Og's eyes began to glaze over.

'Now is the time,' he said in his strange, spectral voice, 'to begin our quest for the Most Fabulous Object in the World, Randall.'

'Og's right!' cried Randall. 'We've still got the map. Let's go!'

'What?' shouted Wally in disbelief. 'Randall, we're in the *middle* of the Atlantic Ocean.'

'There are time-holes in the middle of oceans, too,' Randall insisted.

'You're crazy,' Fidgit said.

'You've just got to trust me,' Randall pleaded.

'That's the problem!'

'Trust the map then,' said Randall. 'It wouldn't have had the Land of Legends on it if it didn't exist.'

'He could be right,' said Strutter and Wally together.

'You're *all* crazy,' said Fidgit.

'We *must* try!' Randall screamed over the raging wind.

'No,' Kevin said, coming into the argument for the first time. 'You're mad!'

'All together now,' Randall cried, 'abandon plank!' He let go, then Wally and Strutter followed. Og let go, too, beaming because everyone seemed to be adopting his suggestion and he didn't even know he'd made it.

'I can't swim!' cried the terrified Fidgit, but he still slipped from the plank leaving only Kevin clinging on and watching in horror as Fidgit gurgled and splashed in the freezing water.

'Hold on, Fidgit,' Kevin cried. 'I'm coming! I'll save you.' Reluctantly, Kevin let go of the sign to go after Fidgit, and it drifted away. 'Randall,' Kevin yelled as he got hold of Fidgit. 'You're crazy!'

At that moment a whirlpool mysteriously formed and sped towards them, faster and faster. Sucked into it, they couldn't stay afloat. All seven were being pulled down by a powerful force . . . and mocking laughter seemed to intermingle with their screams of terror and panic.

In his secret grotto in the Fortress of Ultimate Darkness, Evil wrung his horrible hands and gloated over the Time Bandits' desperate plight.

'Now we have them,' he bragged, to the applause of his cringing minions.

'Oh, well done, your Viciousness,' the toadying Robert said.

Evil laughed his deep and sinister laugh, a bit like coffin-nails being slowly pulled. 'Suddenly, I feel very, very good,' he crowed.

'Oh, I *am* sorry, master,' Benson said understandingly.

'It'll pass,' said Evil, with a wave of his clawed hand.

'Can I bring them in, master?' asked Benson, fawning with malevolent excitement.

'Yes! Yes, Benson, bring the miserable little creatures into the Time of Legends!'

—11—
ON THE OGRE'S MENU

For the longest time – it seemed like hours to Kevin – they were sucked through the murky depths of the freezing water. Kevin was amazed that he seemed to have no trouble breathing. Then quite suddenly they all burst through the surface of the water like seven champagne corks and shot high in the air, only to fall with seven *splooshes* back into the water.

But it wasn't the *same* water at all. Where the North Atlantic around the *Titanic* had been bitterly freezing, this water was warm, warm as bathwater, and strangely buoyant. Kevin and the dwarves weren't so much *in* the water as *on* it. And even stranger, their formal black evening clothes had somehow changed colour. They were now dressed totally in white, from neat bow-ties to patent leather shoes. Even their socks were white.

Fidgit, who had been struggling desperately, suddenly ceased and looked confused. 'Hey,' he called to the others, 'I can swim! I can –'

But everybody was too busy gaping to listen. Coming towards them through the mist was a huge old-fashioned sailing ship. As it listed aimlessly in their direction, tattered sails fitfully filled by the soft, slightly rancid breeze, Kevin thought it looked like a pirate ship from one of his books.

The ship, with its high poopdeck and square-rigged sails, seemed to be half rotten and covered with grey-green fungus. Its tattered sails were black with age and seemed so heavy with dirt that it would take a hurricane to fill them. And hanging from the frayed ropes were bits of meat and bones. Kevin thought they looked like *human* bones. On the foredeck, next to the entrance to the cabin stood a big, black cooking pot on four stumpy legs. There was nobody at the tiller, but the ghostly ship seemed to be steering *directly* towards Kevin and the dwarves.

They all stared and exchanged worried glances. 'Do you think it's a friendly boat?' asked Fidgit, frightened but hopeful.

'Sure,' said Randall with half-hearted optimism. 'Well, probably. We'd better find out.' He raised his short arm towards the ship. 'Hello! Hello!' Kevin and the others joined in a ragged chorus of wishful shouting.

Meanwhile, in the darkened cabin of the peculiar craft, something lay on a heavy carved-oak bed in a heap of filthy rags, snoring like a broken-down carousel. In the dim light all that could be seen, lying on a stained pillow, was a hairy, clawed hand with long nails, gnarled and twisted like small unicorn horns. As it twisted and turned and half opened, the hand seemed to be doing the snoring, and doing it rather badly, too. There was no doubt that this heap was an ogre.

Suddenly, a door was opened into the cabin, and a determined figure marched through the gloom to a hatch and flung it open. A fetid shaft of light sent the snoring hand scuttling into the bedclothes, where it began scratching frantically.

'Good morning, dear,' said Mrs Ogre, moving to a crowded table and beginning to mix a potion in an ancient and encrusted bowl. She was a prim but cheerful woman with deep-green hair knotted tightly at the nape of her neck and a mouth like the slot in a piggy bank. But she looked upon her reluctantly waking husband fondly.

Before the Ogre could answer, the voices of Kevin and the dwarves drifted faintly through the window. 'Help!'

'Wash 'at?' demanded the Ogre, still hidden in the dank darkness of his bed.

'What was what, dear?' asked Mrs Ogre, still stirring as steam rose from the mixing bowl.

'I thought I heard a noise . . . voices,' grumbled the Ogre.

'No, it's just your nerves, dear,' said Mrs Ogre positively. 'Now, sit up and take your potion. You have no idea how late it is.'

'Oooh . . . eurghhh . . . awwwrkk . . . moannn. . .' Whining pitifully, the Ogre sat on the edge of the bed, and for the first time his head came into view. If an ugly contest had been held for ogres, this one, who was called Winston, would have won first prize.

It wasn't that he had a worst feature. *All* of his features were worst. Two scaly horns corkscrewed out of a thick forehead, and his red eyes were like bright and malicious spotlights coming from bottomless wells. A nose like a crooked, hairy mountain rose high over a mouth full of jagged yellow teeth between lips as cruel and relentless as cutlass blades. *And* he had a terrible complexion like the craters of the moon on a murky night. All in all, Winston was very handsome – for an Ogre, that is.

Mrs Ogre moved towards her husband with a frothing beaker. 'Here, dear,' she said soothingly, 'take your potion. Drink it all down. That's a good boy.'

The Ogre drank the potion with a shudder and shook his head. He may have made a disgusted face, but with *his* features, it was hard to tell. 'Grrruuumphhh!' he growled.

'Good, was it dear?' asked Mrs Ogre. 'And now the ointment for your leg. And don't miss any pimples.'

Grumbling and wincing, the Ogre rubbed the sickly green cream into his half-rotting legs while Mrs Ogre began to grind some viper bones in a mortar for her husband's morning medicine.

'Urrrgh . . . owwrhuhnggg . . . awwphht . . .' the Ogre moaned as he applied the ointment. 'I grew too fast when

I was young, that was my problem. I know. . .'

Mrs Ogre came over to him with a bubbling draught in a skull-shaped inhaler. The reason it was skull-shaped was that it *was* a skull. 'Now, inhale deeply,' she demanded sweetly.

'I can't inhale,' the Ogre complained. 'It's bad for my back.'

'But it's good for your throat, dear. Come on. . .'

Reluctantly, Winston closed one nostril with a filthy finger and sniffed deeply, cringing with pain from his back as he did. Then he inhaled with the other nostril. 'I wouldn't have these sore throats if I wasn't an ogre,' he insisted.

'You've been overdoing it, dear, that's all,' soothed Mrs Ogre. Deftly, she began applying ointment to his other leg.

'Be careful,' the Ogre complained. '*You* try being beastly and terrifying and horrible on only one hour's sleep a night because your back hurts, and you don't even dare cough in case you pull a muscle. . .'

'You're horrible to me, dear,' Mrs Ogre said reassuringly.

'You're just saying that,' Winston sulked, but he felt better.

'Now,' she said, holding out a slimy beaker, 'gargle.'

The Ogre took the beaker and poured it into his cruel mouth.

Throwing his head back, he gargled with a roaring, rumbling, appalling noise like a volcano with a bad cold.

'What was *that*?' asked Strutter, treading in watery circles.

'I don't know,' said Randall. 'But maybe we ought to wait for the next boat.'

'Come on!' said Fidgit, and all seven tried frantically to swim away from the nearing craft. But it was like trying to swim in warm tapioca. With raisins.

Back on the ship, the Ogre was going out of the cabin

door with a huge net when he saw himself in the mirror. 'Just look at those spots!' he cried despondently.

'You'll grow out of them, dear,' said Mrs Ogre, though they hadn't got any better in all the time she'd known him.

The Ogre turned from the mirror with a groan, walked up the stairs to the foredeck and prepared to throw his net into the water. 'It's my diet that does it,' he said to himself. 'All this bloody fish. . .' He raised the big net over his head. 'There used to be a time,' he muttered, 'when you could be sure of catching old boots, cans, hat-racks, detergent boxes, dead sheep. Now it's prawns, prawns, prawns all the time. Anti-pollution, phhhaw!' He spat into the sea, causing a small waterspout. With a flick of his mighty but twisted arms and a groan at the pain in his back, the Ogre cast his net far from the ship. There was a splash . . . a cry. The line attached to the net stiffened, and the Ogre hung on to it and began to try to pull it in. More cries came from the misty sea.

'Wife!' called the Ogre. 'Wife! Come up!'

Mrs Ogre appeared from below decks. 'What do you want, dear? The foot powder?'

'No! Come help me – quick!' The Ogre strained to pull in the net, which seemed to be alive and was making struggling and strangled noises.

'What can it be?' asked Mrs Ogre, giving a hand.

'I don't know, but it's not *prawns*! Let's pull!'

'Leave it to me, dear,' she said soothingly. 'Rest your back . . .' With a mighty heave, Mrs Ogre pulled, and as easily as a teabag being pulled from a cup, the net plopped on the slippery deck. In it were Kevin, Randall, the other dwarves, six halibut, three perch, a sunfish and a small squid and a rubber tyre which Vermin immediately grabbed and ate.

Mrs Ogre fell back with surprise. 'Oooh, aren't they lovely?'

Kevin and the Time Bandits, wet, bedraggled and

crushed together, smiled up at Mrs Ogre and tried to look lovely. Their smiles died as Mrs Ogre added: 'We can have them for breakfast!'

'You mean, eat their boots?' Winston asked, his eyes brightening.

'No, dear, eat *all* of them, every scrumptious bit. That is what ogres do, you know.'

'Yes, yes, of course,' agreed the Ogre. 'I forgot.'

'We could have them grilled,' suggested Mrs Ogre.

'Hmmm . . . I don't know,' Winston said doubtfully

'Or minced, with a side salad. Oh, but you don't like salad, do you!'

The Ogre shook his head. 'Nothing in salad,' he proclaimed. 'Just . . . stuff. . .'

'I know!' Mrs Ogre cried. 'Fondue! We haven't had a fondue since you captured that brontosaurus – and that was half a million years ago.'

'Fondue. You mean stick skewers through them and dip them in melted cheese?

'Yes! Let's see . . . we'll need the big pot, and I'll have to sharpen the skewers. It wouldn't do to have blunt skewers.' She turned to bustle back down to the cabin.

'Don't go to any trouble on *our* account,' cried Randall.

'But what shall *I* do?' the Ogre asked.

'Terrify them, of course. You *are* an ogre, you know.'

'I'm *already* terrified,' said Wally. 'Leave me out of it.'

'But what about my you-know-what?' whispered the Ogre, pointing to his bad back.

'You don't have to jump around, dear,' said Mrs Ogre. 'Just shout horribly and leer at them a lot. You know – like you used to do.' She turned back to the doorway, humming cheerfully. 'Oh, this is wonderful!'

Left on his own, the Ogre was less than convinced, but he squared his shoulders manfully. 'Right. Now, let's see.' Screwing his face up painfully, he peered into the Time Bandits' faces, grimacing wildly, and bellowed: "HA HA HA HO!' in a rock-shattering voice. Then, wincing with lower back pain, he knelt down and opened the net. 'Now, let's see what we have here . . . Ha ha! Some tasty little morsels.' He grabbed Fidgit and was just putting him the big black pot when a spasm of pain hit him. Dropping Fidgit with a clang, the Ogre rubbed his tender lumbar region. 'Owww!'

Despite his fear, Kevin couldn't help feeling sorry for the Ogre. Seizing the chance, he asked: 'D–does your back . . . er . . . hurt?'

'What?' roared the Ogre. 'Bad back? Me? An *ogre*? Ha ha! That's ridic–oooh!' he grabbed his back again.

'I know a cure for bad backs,' Kevin hurried on, grabbing at any chance. 'What you need is stretching.'

'Stretching?' demanded the Ogre. 'Certainly not! Nev–oooh!'

Down in the cabin, Mrs Ogre was sharpening some wicked-looking knives and rusty skewers, making sure that they were just the right length for Kevin and each of the dwarves, and humming a happy little fondue song, when from up on deck she heard some very strange noises.

'Heave!' cried seven voices. 'Heave! Heave!'

'Easy now,' begged Winston's voice. 'Easy . . . you'll. . .'

Frowning, Mrs Ogre called out, 'Are they in the pot yet, dear?'

'Just about, darling,' the Ogre called out. 'They're almost there.' To the dwarves he whispered: 'Keep it up! That's better! That's –aaargh! –wonderful!'

If Mrs Ogre could have only witnessed the scene up on deck. Kevin and the dwarves were all out of the net, and the Ogre was flat on his back on the blood-stained deck. Everybody had a grip on an arm or a leg, and they were mightily pulling the horizontal Ogre in opposing directions.

'Heave!' they all cried. 'Heave!'

'Ho!' cried Og.

'You're almost there,' cried the Ogre in ecstasy.

Kevin winked at the others. 'One more time, lads,' he

said. 'Just for luck.' Randall winked back. 'Heave!' they all cried. 'One–two! One–two!'

But instead of stretching the Ogre, they were swinging him back and forth with ever-increasing vigor. 'Right . . . left . . . right!'

'Hey,' cried Winston, 'what's going. . .'

'Left . . . right . . . left . . . right!' called Kevin. 'And over!' With a mighty heave, they gave the Ogre one last swing and threw him over the side into the sea with a mighty splash and an "AAARGHHH!'

'Now, *that's* more like an ogre,' said his wife, as she tested the sharp tip of a skewer below in the cabin, but she didn't like the sound of that splash. 'Winston! What's going on?' she cried, and she began to clump up the stairs.

'Quick!' said Randall up on deck. 'Let's hide in the pot.' Og scrambled in last just as Mrs Ogre came on deck.

'Winston!' she demanded, looking all about but not seeing either her husband or their breakfast. 'Winston!'

'Hey!' called the Ogre from the thick oily, water. 'Is this part of the cure?'

'Winston!' cried Mrs Ogre, moving to the rail of the ship, still fondling a razor-sharp knife. 'What are you doing in the wa–'

Behind her an inverted black iron cooking pot, moved by seven pairs of legs, stealthily across the deck.

'–aaater . . .' continued Mrs Ogre as the cooking pot bumped her into the sea beside her husband. Kevin and the dwarves threw off the pot and cheered as they lined the rail of the ship.

'Well,' spluttered Mrs Ogre as she surfaced. 'I've never had a meal treat me like *that* before! Winston! Are you going to let them get away with. . .'

'My back!' cried the Ogre. 'It's wonderful. I'm cured! I've never felt so free.'

'Get after them!' screeched his wife. 'Winston – you're supposed to be an ogre.'

'I can cough!' shouted Winston. 'At last, I can really

cough!' Filling his mighty chest, he let loose a cough of such force that the noise shattered the atmosphere and filled the ship's sails with wind. Swiftly, the craft was borne away from the dog-paddling Ogre and his irate wife. The Ogre coughed again with delight, and the ship moved even faster.

'There goes our fondue,' said Mrs Ogre. '*And* our boat!'

Strutter grabbed the tiller, and the Ogre's ship was speeding across the water. Randall peered into a telescope. 'We're on the right course,' he said. 'If the wind keeps up, nothing can go wro–'

Suddenly the ship began to lurch from side to side, throwing Vermin, who was gobbling up the remains of a ship's anchor, across the deck.

'Strutter!' Randall cried. 'Keep the rudder straight!'

'It *is* straight!' Strutter shouted. But just then the ship bucked violently as if caught in a hurricane. They all hung on for dear life.

'Drop the mainsail!' called Randall. Grabbing an axe, Wally sliced through the main line, and the huge sail crashed to the deck, but the ship continued to sway uncontrollably.

'All hands on the tiller,' bellowed Randall. All seven of them scrambled to the bridge and grabbed the tiller in a desperate effort to hold the old brig steady, but it still veered wildly.

'Hang on! Hang on!' pleaded Randall. 'Keep her steady.' Slowly, judderingly, the ship seemed to respond. 'That's better. That's better!' But then there was a sound of rushing water, followed by an eerie and total silence. The seven stood mesmerized, wondering what was happening.

Wally, who was standing nearest the rail, looked over the side, and his eyes grew impossibly big. 'Uh, Randall,' he said, 'I . . . I think there's something you should know.' They all crowded to the rail and looked down.

'My God!' said Randall.

As they looked down, they saw that the Ogre's ship was actually rising up out of the water into the sky. The main reason it was doing this was that it was resting on the shaven head of a giant just then striding from the depths of the sea. The ship jerked with every step the giant took and swung perilously as it soared even higher into the sky.

—12—

WHICH WAY TO THE FORTRESS

With every step of the giant's rolling walk, the Ogre's ship swayed alarmingly, and the Time Bandits clung frantically to anything at hand to avoid being thrown to their deaths.

Randall, still clutching the rail for dear life, bellowed commandingly: 'Below decks! Everybody below decks!' Looking around to see if he was being obeyed, Randall was amazed to find that the dwarves had already *gone* below.

'Come on!' Kevin beckoned impatiently from the doorway.

In a single bound, Randall was off the bridge and down in the cabin among the huddled Time Bandits.

Meanwhile, the giant's steps were taking him closer to the shore. Slowly his massive body, rolling with baby fat, began to rise out of the water.

Ahead, peaceful and unsuspecting, an unhappy troll, a small pink-skinned creature with rubbery features and pale sticking-up hair, sat outside his tumbledown cottage by the shore. From inside the cottage came the cry of a baby troll which, as anybody who knows trolls can testify, is an awesome combination of air-raid siren and concrete mixer. Since troll babies sleep only one hour out of twenty-four and spend the rest of the time crying, the troll had heard quite enough of it.

Things were made worse by the fact that, as the giant's giant steps took him inexorably towards the troll's little cottage, Mrs Troll kept popping out not only to get away from Baby Troll, but to give her husband a piece of her rather common mind.

'It's all your fault,' she screamed as unheeded the giant drew closer.

'Ah,' said the troll disgustedly, 'go fry your elbows.'

As Mrs Troll dashed back into the hovel to try to howl the baby into a moment of silence, Mr Troll leaned against a glum tree and tried to think of fifteen reasons why he'd got married in the first place. He was still stuck on number one when the giant's huge hips cleared the water, and his head, still jauntily wearing the Ogre's ship, disappeared into the fleecy clouds overhead.

The noise from inside the cottage, what with Baby Troll howling lustily and Mrs Troll trying to drown him out, sounded like overtime in the boiler works, and Mr Troll sighed and thought fondly about the time his father had been turned into a doorknocker by an evil witch. Those were the good old days.

In a moment, Mrs Troll returned, her mission a complete failure. If she hadn't been so busy scolding her husband and compiling a complete list of thirty years of sins, misdemeanours and oversights on his part, she might have noticed that the sea was now only up to the giant's knees, and he was heading directly towards their happy home. Even then, the shadow of his great boat-wearing head had entered their untidy garden.

The ground around them shook slightly with each step the giant took on the shore, but Mrs Troll was too busy to notice, and Mr Troll had his back to both his wife and the giant. But Baby Troll must have sensed that something was up, for he redoubled his wailing. The volume rose and rose until the unhappy troll pressed both of his hands over his ears in an effort to block out the terrific din.

It was while the troll was so occupied that the giant's long steps brought his broad foot directly down on the troll's house with a horrible KKKRRRUUUNNNCCCHHH!

As the unmindful giant strode inland, the troll removed his hands from his ears and was delighted to hear nothing but silence. Wonderful silence. *Silent* silence. Mr Troll lit up his old briar pipe and sighed: 'Ah, that's better.'

Meanwhile, up in the clouds around the giant's head, Kevin and the dwarves were bouncing off the sides of the cabin and wondering how they were ever going to get down alive. A high-flying pterodactyl smashed into the side of the ship, scaring them even more.

'Quick,' said Randall, getting an idea, 'start tearing up the floorboards. We've got to try to stop him somehow!'

The dwarves all grabbed the Ogre's instruments of torture and began prising up the half-rotten boarding of the ship's floor. Pushing aside a thick layer of bleached bones, they soon exposed a great, warty section of the giant's bald head. The warts were the size of small cannonballs.

'*Now* what shall we do?' cried Fidgit.

'Hit him!' cried Randall, grabbing a sledge hammer which just happened to by leaning against a bulkhead and swinging it mightily over his head. The heavy hammer descended forcefully, but bounced off the giant's bald pate as if it were made of rubber. Getting into the spirit of things, Og began jumping up and down on the giant's skull and chanting: 'Take that! Take that! Take that!'

'If he was a bit smaller,' Vermin said, 'I'd eat him.'

Below, the strolling giant rolled his eyes up and felt as though someone were tickling his scalp. Sticking a finger up between the Ogre's ship and his head, he scratched, rocking the ship and the Time Bandits inside from side to side violently. Then he smiled contentedly and lowered his hand.

'Here,' said Randall, when he'd regained his feet and grabbed a coil of rope. 'Tie this around my waist and lower me down. I've got to find out what this big fellow is all about.' With Kevin and the other five holding on to the other end of the rope, Randall carefully slipped down through the hull of the ship on to the giant's head.

'Slowwwly!' he cautioned them, holding on to a wart and letting himself slowly down the bristly but slick surface. What few hairs the giant had on his head were like huge spikes and very pointed.

Soon Randall was down to the top of a huge, pointed ear the size of a three-storey house. 'A little lower,' he whispered, and the others let him down a few more feet.

Now Randall was level with the huge ear, which sprouted a luxuriant jungle of hair. He was about to order his helpers to lower him even further when he happened to glance into the giant's ear and, to his surprise, saw a light in it. Randall swung himself in until he could stand on the lower lobe of the giant's ear and look directly into it. To his surprise, in the distance beyond the dense growth of spiky hair, he saw blue sky and little bits of cloud through the giant's other ear. Then suddenly he glanced down and saw the giant's hand slowly rising as if to scratch his ear.

'Up! Up!' Randall cried in a panic. 'Pull me up!'

Kevin and the dwarves heaved, and soon Randall was back in the Ogre's ship, panting and sweating and practically unable to speak.

'But what are we going to do now?' asked Fidgit.

Looking around the crowded and murky cabin, Kevin decided on another line of attack. High above them was the Ogre's medicine chest, and there, among jars labelled 'Eye of Newt', 'Toe of Bat' and 'Dessicated Wombat's Blood', was a big, cobwebby bottle with 'Super Sleeping Elixir' written on it.

Climbing up on a rickety ladder, Kevin brought down the elixir bottle and looked around again. There, leaning against the old iron cooker, was a set of bellows with a long spout. Pouring the sleeping potion into the bellows, and squirting a bit into the air to make sure that it came out, he returned to where the giant's bald head gleamed dully below the broken floor of the boat.

'Hold on to the back of my coat,' Kevin told Og and Wally, and he leaned carefully over the big expanse of naked scalp. Finding just the right spot between a freckle and a mole, Kevin inserted the sharp end of the spout into the giant's scalp with a powerful jab. With all his strength, he squeezed the bellows, forcing the sleeping elixir into the top of the giant's head.

'*Now* what?' asked Wally.

Below them, the giant reacted as if he'd been bitten by a mosquito. Frowning, he rolled his great eyes upward with annoyance. The wrinkling of his brow caused the ship to jump, throwing the Time Bandits in every direction at once. The ship resettled at a slightly sharper angle, leaving Kevin and the dwarves all lying in a jumbled heap in one corner of the cabin.

But the sleeping elixir was definitely taking effect. Yawning mightily, the giant raised fists the size of small mountains and rubbed them into his eyes. He took another couple of hundred-yard steps, but then stumbled, shaking the Time Bandits like peas in a saucepan. Falling asleep on his feet, the giant fell to his knees, and the ship on his head dropped like a lift gone berserk. Rocking woozily back and forth, the drugged giant put his hands on the ground and then fell flat on his face. The ship with the Time Bandits slid off his head into a muddy field, coming to a jerking halt and scrambling Kevin and the dwarves like so many eggs.

Peering out of the cabin porthole, the Time Bandits saw that the giant was soundly asleep, his whistling snores filling the sails of the firmly grounded ship. With subdued shouts of joy, they scrambled up on deck, jumped off the ship, and ran as fast as they could until they were swallowed up in a misty wood. Behind them, the giant rolled over fitfully in his sleep, crushing the Ogre's boat.

It seemed to the Time Bandits as though they were running for days, but by the time Kevin paused to draw breath, the snores of the subterranean giant had receded, and apart from the panting of a half-dozen breathless dwarves and a peculiar cracking noise from Vermin's mouth, all was quiet. Deathly quiet. It was as though a blanket had descended upon them, muffling all sound, like snow on a winter's morning. Kevin looked up and was surprised to see that the rocky landscape and its thousand-year-old oak trees had quite disappeared. Instead there was emptiness. Nothing for miles in front and nothing for miles behind. It was very odd and a little frightening. The sun was big and high and bright green in the sky.

Wally was the first to break the silence. 'Let's stop for a minute, Randall . . .' he grunted. He was sweating. They all were. And it wasn't even very hot. For some unaccountable reason they were all scared.

'Where are we . . .?' asked Fidgit nervously, passing his tongue over the front of a dry mouth.

Randall, who had pulled out the map again, was hardly reassuring. 'Don't worry,' he said, 'I think I know . . .'

'I'm tired, Randall,' was all Kevin could say. His legs felt like lead weights.

'Ah!' Randall spoke with sudden decisive authority. 'Right, then right again.' And with that he made two sharp turns to the right. No one could see why, but it seemed the thing to do, and for want of better orders, the small, tired band made two quick right turns in the middle of nowhere. This short burst of activity revived their spirits temporarily, but a second later, Fidgit suddenly screamed and reeled back, pointing at the ground as if he'd trodden on a puff adder and three friends.

It was a shock, though, to see the bleached bones of a semi-human skeleton half covered in the sand, and a rotting skull cracked by Fidgit's unwary foot.

'Bones,' said Randall, dismissively. . . . 'You've seen bones before.'

'Usually they have skin over them, Randall,' pointed out Wally heavily.

'Ow!' yelled Strutter.

They all turned. Strutter lay where he had stumbled, tripped by a half-unearthed rib-cage, and beyond that shoulder-blades of some enormous creature. Jaw-bones and collar-bones and pelvises and femurs – there were old bones everywhere. The gang were thoroughly unnerved now. All except for Vermin who beamed and licked his lips and was about to bend down and start on the first course when, with a sharp boot up the back side, Randall propelled him along with the rest.

'Come on!' shouted Randall. 'We've got to keep going.'

'But *where* . . . ?' protested Kevin. It all looked exactly the same as far as the eye could see.

'To the Fortress of Ultimate Darkness, you little fool . . . to the Most Fabulous Object In the World!'

'You don't still believe in all that Randall . . . surely?' Kevin retorted with weary and frustrated bitterness.

Randall strode on, tapping the map with an almost hysterical intensity. He looked a little mad from where Kevin was standing.

'It says on the map,' he shouted, 'we're nearly there!'

Vigorously and determinedly, he stalked off in the direction of the farthest horizon but he had not gone more than a half dozen yards when a most peculiar thing happened. Randall stopped. Not falteringly or uncertainly . . . he smack bang wallop stopped so hard he was nearly knocked off his feet. But what made it all the more extraordinary was that there was absolutely nothing to stop him. The long flat empty plain stretched ahead unbroken, and yet for some reason, Randall could not move another inch forward.

Kevin and the others ran up beside him and they too found themselves brought to a sharp bruising standstill by absolutely nothing. They pushed and shoved and tried everything, but they only ended up with their noses pressed hard against the invisible barrier, beyond which stretched the interminable flatness.

Wally turned on Randall angrily. 'What's all this about?'

'*I* don't know,' Randall snapped back.

'Look on the map.'

'It's not *on* the map!' shouted Randall bitterly, and turning on his heel stalked away from the others.

'We're going to die,' moaned Fidgit.

'Rubbish,' muttered Randall, but he didn't sound very convinced as he turned the map this way and that.

But Fidgit was thoroughly rattled by now. He screamed at Randall. 'No one gets out of here alive, Randall . . . don't you understand . . . can't you see!' He jabbed his finger in the direction of the litter of bones.

At that Randall finally lost what little control he may have had, and with a violent shriek of anger that was halfway between a parrot being sick and a Black and Decker drill, he grabbed a skull from the ground and hurled it at Fidgit with all his might. Fidgit ducked. The skull missed his skull by inches and flew past until it struck the invisible barrier. The barrier shattered in a thousand pieces. The gang crouched fearfully down, not daring to look. When they *did* look they saw Randall staring behind them, mouth wide open, eyes bulging in amazement. He seemed to be trying to say something but couldn't. Slowly they turned and there, not a few hundred yards from where they were standing, where once there had been nothing at all, stood the mighty bulk of a strange and forbidding castle.

Randall quickly unrolled the map. That's it,' he cried excitedly. 'Yes! It's the Fortress of Ultimate Darkness.'

'Not quite,' said Og in his mechanical voice.

'What?' cried Randall. 'But. . .'

'Look!' urged Og, pointing even further up into the troubled sky.

They all craned their necks to follow his gesture, and to their amazement they found that the castle was but a gatehouse to an even more fabulous structure stretching endlessly, a smooth, black column, into the very clouds themselves. The black façade of glistening marble was split by a gaping crack which widened grotesquely as it reached for unseen heights.

'There,' said Og in his peculiar voice, 'we shall find the Most Fabulous Object in the World,' and he lurched forward.

The others, hypnotized by unimaginable greed, followed Og as if tied to him by invisible bonds. Only Kevin's face showed doubt and deep disquiet. But he, too, followed. The malignant light of the moon suddenly shone on their upraised and greedy faces.

Evil, in his grotto, thrust his hand into the magic pool and destroyed the image. 'They have found us at last,' he cackled. 'Now let them approach,' he said. 'Poor miserable wretches.' He laughed horribly, and his minions joined in a patter of polite applause.

—13—

THE MOST FABULOUS OBJECT IN THE WORLD

High up at a tiny window on the wall of the almost endlessly tall castle, Benson watched as Kevin and the Time Bandits crept greedily up to the entrance of the gatehouse.

'Here they are, master,' he shrieked over his shoulder.

'Don't be boring, Benson,' said Evil, 'I know that.'

Below, a broad drawbridge lowered itself before the Time Bandits' feet. 'Don't you think,' asked Kevin worriedly, 'that this is turning out to be just a little bit too easy?'

'You've got a suspicious mind, Kevin,' said Randall as they cautiously crept across the creaking drawbridge. 'That's your problem.'

Just as the last of them – Fidgit, as usual – stepped off the drawbridge on to the other side, it suddenly shuddered, cracked and fell into an apparently bottomless moat, thus cutting off any possible retreat.

Wally was the first to reach the great double doors leading into the citadel. At first they were stiff, but when all seven pushed, the doors creaked open with an eerie wail, and they stopped wide-eyed and looked cautiously into a vast, deserted entrance hall. There was no sign of life anywhere. The floor was thick with dust undisturbed for centuries. The odd bone stuck out of the debris of the ages, and they sensed that this was a place of eternal darkness.

Instinctively, they all stopped, but Randall urged them

forward. 'Come on,' he said, 'we're almost there.' Reluctantly they pressed forward, leaving a trail of footprints in the thick dust.

But then Strutter chanced to look back and to notice that, as they walked, their footprints were disappearing as if they were walking in water.

'Look, Randall!' he said.

'It's just a trick of the light,' said Randall. 'Listen to this. Hallllooo!' he cried. 'Anybody there?'

There was no answer but many echoes of Randall's voice as it bounced off the impossibly high walls. 'See?' said Randall. 'Nothing to be scared of.'

Soon they turned a corner into an even *larger* hall, in the middle of which was a great mountain of rubble. As Vermin scrambled up it looking for something edible, he grabbed a skeletal arm which came away in his hands setting off a great rumbling and shaking high above their heads. As the terrified Vermin tumbled down the mountain of debris, dust and chunks of masonry fell all about them, and a fluted marble column crashed directly in front of them.

A great jagged shaft of light raced across the floor of the hall and up the far wall. Looking in the direction of the light, the Time Bandits saw that it was pouring out of a gigantic crack in one of the walls. Music also flowed from the opening – bright, lively, entrancing music which seemed to promise them everything. As one, the gang rushed forward scrambling through the opening that led to the light.

On the other side, they stopped awestruck, rubbing their eyes at the magnificence before them. An even more enormous hall was ablaze with light, and in the middle of it was a towering pillar of perspex and chromium, multicoloured fluorescent tubing and gleaming plastic, absolutely throbbing with radiance. And at its very top, glistening in the light of thousands of baby spotlights, was what *must* have been the Most Fabulous Object in the World.

At that distance, in that bright light, it was impossible o tell exactly what the Most Fabulous Object was. Its heer radiance created a blinding light which dazzled the ye and clouded the mind with desire, but each of the lwarves was certain that he was at last seeing the object of ais dreams and fantasies. Their minds throbbed with its nany desirable qualities.

'Wow!' said Randall. 'A self-lighting dial!'

'Easy-wipe surfaces!' exulted Wally.

'Recessed knobs and foolproof controls,' babbled Og, vho seemed to be himself again.

'Ninety-nine harmonious colours and flavours,' lrooled Vermin.

'Computerized, remote-controlled, miniaturized . . .' ighed Strutter.

'Bigger! . . . smaller! . . . lighter! . . . sturdier! . . . *ortable*!' exulted Fidgit.

Suddenly, high above their heads, a platform jutted out rom the middle of the obelisk, and on it were a forty-ight-piece orchestra and a figure Kevin remembered rom the television set at home. It was the compère from Your Money Or Your Life'. His teeth, suit, hair, eyes nd shoes gleamed with an unearthly radiance. The rchestra burst into a catchy tune, and the compère's mile lit up like a neon sign. He opened his arms wide to velcome the Time Bandits.

'And here they are! Ladies and gentlemen, the proud vinners of the Most Fabulous Object in the World. The nswer to all their problems – and *yours* – is here! For *hem – tonight*!'

Suddenly, lights flared behind Kevin and the dwarves, nd they were in a vast television studio complete with an udience cheering wildly and pointing at the Most abulous Object in the World.

'Us?' cried the delighted dwarves, mesmerized by the rospect of at last attaining their hearts' desire. '*Us*?'

'Yes,' exulted the compère, 'you! The Time Bandits!'

As the studio audience went mad behind them, a se of broad stairs began to descend from the compère' platform, extending down to the dwarves and Kevin and a diamond-bright spotlight picked them out from o high.

The compère, a microphone in his hand, began walkin down the stairs, and he was joined from behind by Mr an Mrs Lotterby, Kevin's parents. His father was dazzling i a gold lamé sports jacket and white trousers, and Kevin' mother was dressed exactly like a Las Vegas chorus girl right up to the ostrich plume rising from her brilliantl blonde hair. Their smiles were dazzling, and the beckoned to Kevin and the dwarves.

'No!' cried Kevin, but the dwarves, maddened by gree for the Most Fabulous Object in the World and dazzled b the glamour, rushed to the foot of the steps just as th compère, flanked by Mr and Mrs Lotterby, came dow the last few steps. The compère made a broad gestur and, high above, the Most Fabulous Object began to floa towards them, growing in radiance as it descended.

Closer and closer it came, but so incandescent was th Most Fabulous Object that although it got bigger an bigger, it never became any clearer. To each of the Tim Bandits it appeared differently. No two of them coul even agree what colour it was. But it obviously *was* th Most Fabulous Object in the World. It was wonderfu even worth dying for.

As the Most Fabulous Object grew so close that it wa literally hovering over the dwarves' heads, only Kevi held back. The dwarves craned their necks to stare up int its brilliance. Their features had turned into masks of pur greed.

Reaching the bottom step right in front of them, th compère held out his hand and said: 'And now, as th possessors of the Most Fabulous Object in the World, don't suppose you'll have any more use for that tatty ol map. May I have it, please?'

'Yes! yes! Go on!' cried the audience, and almost as if he were in a dream, Randall held out the map and put it into the compère's hand.

Suddenly, the Most Fabulous Object in the World plunged over the heads of the dwarves and became a sturdy, iron cage trapping them inside. The compère instantly became Evil, and Kevin's parents were replaced by Robert and Benson. The audience quickly became a multitude of demons, monsters and evil beasts and then disappeared completely along with the television studio. Only Evil, Robert and Benson were left.

'I have the map! Today I have the map!' cackled Evil, holding it high in a taloned hand. 'And the day after tomorrow . . . the World! And I have *them*!' he added, pointing to the imprisoned dwarves. Turning his gaze on Kevin, he told Robert and Benson, 'Throw the kid in with them and hang them all over the bottomless abyss for a few eternities.'

Robert and Benson may not have been the brightest helpers, but it wasn't very long before Kevin and the Time Bandits found themselves hanging in the iron-barred cage over a bottomless black abyss. They had never seen so much bottomlessness. No one felt very cheerful, so they just sat there looking listlessly at two similar cages hanging nearby. In a way it would have been nice to have company, but the other cages were full of the fleshless bones of Evil's prisoners who'd been there for some considerable time.

Nobody spoke until Vermin, who had been carefully watching a rat climbing down the heavy rope which supported the great metal cage, suddenly snaked out his hand and grabbed it. 'Rat, anybody?' he asked politely.

'No thanks, Vermin,' said Fidgit. Nobody else bothered to answer.

'Might be the last meal we'll get,' muttered Vermin, eyeing the rat distastefully. The rat was doing the same to him.

Strutter finally stopped staring at the floor of the cage and said: 'Well, I guess that's it, then.'

'It's all over,' agreed Wally.

'How could we have been so *stupid*?' moaned Fidgit.

'I dunno,' said Og.

Randall, who felt responsible for getting the Time Bandits into such a mess, didn't say a thing for a change.

Nor did Kevin, who was slumped in one corner of the cage, tears in his eyes, looking at one of the Polaroid photographs he'd taken of King Agamemnon in Mycenae. How he wished he were back in the palace just then, or that Agamemnon could somehow come to his rescue. Idly he looked at another couple of photographs from Mycenae, then picked up one he'd taken of the dwarves flaunting Napoleon's treasure in Sherwood Forest. He started to go on to another Greek scene, but then excitedly looked back to the group photo.

Rummaging hurriedly in his school satchel, Kevin came up with his magnifying glass and examined the photo again very carefully. Then he jumped to his feet and scrambled over to Randall and the others.

'Hey,' he said excitedly. 'Look at this!'

The dwarves gathered around without much enthusiasm to look at the photograph. 'Good one of Wally,' said Fidgit.

'No,' said Kevin, 'look carefully.'

They all looked more closely, but just grunted uncomprehendingly.

'The map!' insisted Kevin. 'Look at the map in Randall's hands.'

'We can see the map,' said Randall impatiently, 'but why rub it in? We don't *have* it any more.'

'Look closer with my magnifying glass,' said Kevin. 'There's the Time of Legends, and right in the middle of it the Fortress of Ultimate Darkness. . .'

'Yeah,' said Strutter. 'So what?'

'Well, look right below it.'

Randall gave a low whistle of amazement. 'That's a time-hole!'

'Yes!'

'And look at the size of it,' said Randall admiringly.

'Exactly!' said Kevin.

'It must lead *any*where.'

'Everywhere . . .' said Kevin.

'What?' said Strutter.

Randall jumped to his feet with excitement. 'Gang,' he said, 'we've just found the biggest time-hole in the universe, and it's practically right under our feet. Kevin, you're a genius. Come on, you lot,' he exhorted, 'let's shift!'

'We'll never get out of here,' said Fidget sadly.

'Want to bet?' said Og, springing into action.

'That's it, Og,' said Randall. 'We'll show them we can do *something* right.'

Og was already studying the lock on the iron cage. Grabbing Kevin's satchel, he dumped its contents on the floor of the cage and began to rummage. He came up with the beautiful knife which Agamemnon had given Kevin. Sadly, but realizing that it was in a good cause, Kevin watched as Og jammed the knife into the lock and twisted it around violently. After much bending and turning of the knife the cage door sprang open. Kevin's precious souvenir of Mycenae now resembled a corkscrew.

Randall snatched the knife from Og's hands and passed it to Fidgit, who scrambled up the outside of the swinging cage to the top and began cutting strands from the thick rope cable holding it up. One by one, he dropped the strands down to Wally and Strutter, who began to braid them. Before very long, they had a long, thin rope, but the cable holding the cage was getting extremely frayed and looked in danger of snapping at any moment.

They tied the newly braided rope around Strutter's waist and lowered him from the cage. Slowly, they began to swing Strutter back and forth, farther and farther, until with a final effort he flew into space and grabbed on to the neighbouring cage. 'Ping!' went the weakened cable above them as another strand snapped.

Strutter clung desperately to the bars of the second cage while the other end of the rope was tied around Wally's waist. Then moving to the door of their prison, Wally checked his angle carefully and leaped into the void, arcing under Strutter's cage and barely reaching the third cage. No sooner had Wally firmly grasped its bars than Strutter let go and swung under Wally and on to the firm rock at the edge of the bottomless abyss.

The Time Bandits all cheered as Strutter tied the rope to a stone column, but at the same time, another menacing 'Twoiiinnnggg!' sounded as yet another strand of the cable snapped. Quickly, Wally untied himself from the middle of the rope, and it was pulled taut between the cage the other four were in and the stone column. One by one, Vermin, Fidgit, Og, Kevin, then Randall slid down the rope to safety, but as they did so another strand of the hawser broke, and the first cage was literally hanging by a thread.

Wally measured his position and fearlessly let go of the third cage, dropping towards the taut line. But just as he grabbed it, the weakened cable parted with a 'SNAP!' and the first cage, the rope *and* Wally plummeted into the bottomless abyss. The Time Bandits flinched as Wally's wail of terror died in the remote depths. Then all was quiet, and the only evidence that the cage or Wally had ever existed was the strand of rope leading from the stone column down into the abyss.

Kevin and the other Time Bandits looked at each other with shocked eyes, too stunned to speak. Could that be the last they would ever see of Wally? Then suddenly Fidgit pointed with excitement and tried to speak: 'L–l–loo–k,' he gasped. The rope leading down over the precipice was twitching! As one, they all grabbed hold of it and pulled and heaved until, finally, Wally, grinning like a madman, was pulled up over the edge of the stone, and he still had Kevin's mangled Grecian knife between his teeth.

'We've done it!' cried Randall, as they all hugged Wally with relief.

'Hurrah!' cried all the others, but they sobered quickly when Kevin said:

'Now all we need is the map.'

'What?' said Randall. 'Are you crazy?'

'We've got to get the map,' repeated Kevin.

'Don't be a fool,' said Randall. 'We know where the time-hole is. Let's get out of here.'

He started to lead the others away, but Kevin grabbed his arm. 'Randall,' he said, 'Evil's got the map!'

'Damned right he has,' said Randall, 'and the last thing I want to do is see *him* again. Come on!' He started to go again, but Kevin stood firmly in the way.

'But we can't leave him with that map,' he insisted. 'He'll destroy the world.'

—14—

IN THE GRIP OF EVIL

In his grotto, the triumphant Evil was poring over the map and plotting his inexorable conquest of the world, beginning with the replacement of butterflies, babbling brooks and sweet-smelling little babies by silicon chips, motorized roller-skates and disposable grandmothers.

'Oh, Benson,' he exulted, 'I feel the power of evil coursing through my veins, filling every cranny of my being with the desire to do wrong, absolute wrong! I feel *so* bad, Benson.'

'Good, master, good!' encouraged Benson, happy to see his sovereign back in his old form.

'Yes, it *is* good,' Evil said. 'For this is the best – I mean worst – sort of badness I am feeling.'

'Kill me!' moaned Benson. 'Kill me, master!'

'Not yet, Benson,' Evil said regretfully. 'We have much work to do . . . no less a work than to overthrow creation itself. We will remake man in *my* image; we will turn the mountains into seas. . .'

Outside the great door to Evil's grotto, Kevin was peering through the keyhole while the others lurked in the shadows, ready to make a break for it at any moment.

'This is madness,' whispered Randall.

'. . . And we will make the seas into fire,' Evil continued, 'and the fire into a mighty rushing wind that will cover the face of the earth and wipe clean the scourge of woolly thinking once and for all. . .'

'Here,' said Randall, pushing Kevin aside and looking

through the keyhole. 'Let *me* see.'

'And . . . and . . . and,' said Benson, trying to equal his master's passionate sense of evil mission, 'we can turn . . . beans into peas!'

'Ah, Benson, dear Benson,' Evil said fondly, 'you are so mercifully free of the ravages of intelligence.'

'You say such nice things, master.'

'Yes,' said Evil. 'I'm sorry. Now, Benson, Robert and I have important work to do, so I'm going to turn you into a dog for a while . . . a nasty, black, rabid dog with several varieties of fleas and bad breath.'

'Oh, thank you, master,' rejoiced Benson.

There was a mighty flash of light which drove Randall and Kevin back from the keyhole, and sure enough, a black, yellow-eyed mongrel now sat on the table next to the map, foaming at the mouth and snarling.

'Guard the map, Benson,' commanded Evil. 'Or else!'

'Meow!' said Benson, not being particularly bright as a dog, either.

Evil snapped his fingers and Robert, who made up in machine-like imbecility what he lacked of Benson's flair for idiocy, lurched to his side. Together they stared into the video pool.

'Robert,' said Evil, 'we must plan a New World together. . .'

'Grunt,' agreed Robert.

'. . . but this time we will start properly. Tell me what you know about computers.'

'Well,' began Robert, 'a computer is an automatic electronic apparatus for making calculations or controlling operations that are expressible in numerical or logical terms. . .'

'Go on,' crowed Evil, 'I like it!'

Behind them, the door to the grotto slowly opened, and Kevin beckoned to the others to follow him.

'And fast-breeder reactors?' Evil demanded. 'What about them?'

'I'm glad you asked that,' said Robert. 'Fast-breeder reactors use a fast fission process for the generation of fissile isotopes. . .'

The dwarves all tiptoed into the grotto behind Kevin as quietly as they could, but Benson stopped scratching behind his ear and growled menacingly. The Time Bandits vanished behind a pillar.

'Quiet, Benson,' said Evil off-handedly. 'Show me more, Robert. Show me more. Show me subscriber trunk dialling . . . automated stock control . . . chickenless egg production. I must know *everything*!'

The dwarves tried again to move towards the map on the table, but again Benson growled, and the hackles on his scruffy neck rose. Looking about him, Kevin noticed a skeleton chained to the wall with a mail-order catalogue where it used to have a lap. Stealthily, Kevin reached for a leg bone and then flung it with all of his might into a far corner of the grotto.

Benson, after a split second of wondering whether this might not be a trick to get him away from the map, jumped off the table and raced into the darkness in search of the bone. Stupid Benson!

Kevin motioned, and Og and Vermin moved swiftly forward towards the table. Og vaulted over Vermin's shoulders on to the table and scooped up the rolled map, neatly tossing it to Randall who threw it to Kevin near the door.

'Quick!' shouted Kevin, motioning to the dwarves to run through the doorway. But hearing the scuffling, Evil whipped around and saw that the map was gone.

'Stop!' he screamed, raising a long-taloned finger.

All of the Time Bandits had escaped from the grotto except for Og, who had slipped and fallen by the door. Evil, eyes blazing with malice, bent back his long fingernails in rapid succession, and a stream of rockets flew towards the door. Og was just scrambling to his feet when he disappeared in a cloud of tiny explosions. With superhuman effort, he lunged towards the door.

The others were all outside when Og managed to career through the door, but he wasn't the same Og, at least not from the waist up. Above the belt, Og had been turned into a fat little pink pig. On the pig's long-snouted head was Og's Viking helmet with only one horn.

'Og!' cried the others.

'Oink!' squealed Og, as confused as they were.

But there was no time to waste. Grabbing Og by his cloven hoof, Kevin raced down the dark and sinister hallway with the others close behind.

'After them!' howled Evil in his grotto. 'Stop them by every means in my *power*!'

The Time Bandits dashed into the darkness with the sound of ever-closer footsteps echoing behind them and thunderbolts zapping overhead and exploding in the distance. A wind began to howl around them, pulling at their clothing, and strange, swirling lights converged on them from the heights.

Suddenly the stone floor in front of the fleeting Time Bandits erupted, and a swarm of horrific, fantastic-headed ghouls swarmed up through the broken stone to block the way out of the Fortress of Ultimate Darkness. Sliding and stumbling desperately, the gang turned down a dark side passage, but in the distance Kevin could see other hordes of long-robed ghouls converging on them.

'We'll have to split up,' Kevin shouted, 'or they'll get us all.' He held the rolled-up map tightly in his hand. 'The map is what he wants. You guys make a dash for the time-hole and try to get some help – any help, from anywhere – hurry! I'll draw them away. Evil won't do anything that will destroy the map, so maybe I can hold them off for a while.'

'You can't stay alone,' insisted Wally.

'All right,' agreed Kevin, 'I'll take one other of –' But they had all disappeared into the darkness except Og, who stood beside Kevin panting heavily and making pig-like noises.

'Come on!' shouted Kevin, grabbing Og by the hoof again and dragging him into yet another dark corridor as a fireball whizzed over their heads and the baying, sinister shapes behind them grew closer and closer. The sides of the craggy corridor grew ever narrower and Kevin and the half-pig plunged down it blindly.

At the end of the corridor, which was now so narrow that Og and Kevin had to go single-file, was a tall door, and with a terrified glance behind them, Kevin pushed Og squealing through the doorway and stumbled after him.

They were suddenly in a colossal hall made up of contrasting slabs of coloured marble like a giant draughts board. Great piles of stone blocks loomed menacingly over them, and overhead a large chunk of the ceiling had collapsed and light streamed in through the jagged opening. In the centre of this pool of light stood Evil, with Robert fawning at his shoulder. Evil had a long arm raised, a taloned finger pointing directly at Kevin. Kevin glanced behind him, but the narrow doorway was full of Evil's ghouls. All retreat was cut off, so the small boy and the demi-pig who used to be Og turned wearily to face the triumphant Evil. Kevin clutched the map even harder.

'You are a very troublesome little fellow,' Evil snarled at Kevin. 'I think I should teach you one of my special lessons.' Robert sniggered ingratiatingly by his side. 'What do you think, Robert?' Evil continued. 'What would be appropriate? Shall I make him half donkey, half warthog or. . .'

'Master! Master!' Robert pleaded, 'turn him into half wombat and half . . . er . . . er . . . half – wombat!' He paused, scratching his head and wondering if that could be exactly right.

'No, I've got it, I'll make this little nuisance half oyster and half goat . . . no . . . perhaps he'd like to be half mouldy carrot, half schoolmaster!'

Behind Og and Kevin, the ghouls laughed knowingly,

but Evil had stopped smiling and was advancing with a long arm outstretched and his terrifying eyes staring directly into Kevin's 'Enough of pleasantries,' he growled, 'give me that map.'

But quickly Kevin snatched a torch from a holder on the crumbling wall and held it dangerously close to the rolled map. Evil fell back a step with a snarl of rage.

'Call off those . . . those creatures,' Kevin demanded, 'or I'll destroy the map forever!'

'Don't be so. . .' Evil began, starting forward again.

'Call them off!' Kevin insisted, bringing the torch so close to the map that one edge of it began to smoke.

'Very well,' said Evil disagreeably. 'Who needs them, anyway?' With a flick of his wrist, a bolt of lightning streaked over Kevin's head and struck the clustered ghouls who crowded the doorway behind him. The ghouls instantly began to melt like so many wax figures, their horrible features crumbling and running into a flaming pool on the floor which glimmered faintly and then went out entirely. A huge bubble rose to the surface of the pool and broke, releasing a smell of rotten cabbage.

'Him, too!' commanded Kevin, pointing the now-glowing map at Robert.

'If you insist,' Evil said, arching his eyebrows. He turned to his faithful servant. 'Robert, your time has come.'

'Oh, wonderful, wonderful,' Robert cried. 'Thank you, master.'

'But before I destroy you, I'd like you to know, Robert that I never liked you . . . never! Not . . . one . . . tiny . . . bit!'

'Oh, your Trickyness,' Robert began gratefully, 'thank–'

But before he could finish, a cracking flash of light encircled Robert and he exploded with a mighty roar, then another and another. Bits of Robert shot high into the vast hall, bursting with ever more elaborate displays of pyrotechnics until finally a glorious starburst rained bits of phosphorescence Robert down on the chequered floor. Robert was no more.

'You see,' Evil said suavely, 'I am a reasonable man. Give me the map and you may at least walk out of here on human feet.'

'No!' said Kevin. 'No!'

Evil stretched out his long-nailed hand and, almost as an afterthought, sent a burst of white-hot energy flashing towards Og. Suddenly the bottom half of Og was turned into pig, too, and he ran squealing into the darkness.

'And now,' Evil said, closing in on Kevin. His arm went up, and Kevin screamed and fell to the floor. When he looked up, Kevin saw Evil leering in triumph, the map held aloft in one cruel hand. Slowly, elaborately, Evil brought his other hand up and then pointed it down at the cringing Kevin.

There was an almighty crash and Kevin, thinking that his time had come, instinctively closed his eyes and prepared for the end. But nothing happened. All was stunned silence. Warily, Kevin opened his eyes and looked up, to see Evil frozen with arm uplifted and staring behind him, his mouth working silently in astonishment.

—5—
TIME BANDITS TO THE RESCUE

As Kevin looked behind him in amazement, a huge Sherman tank with Randall at the controls continued to plough through the chequered wall of the great hall, its long cannon pointing directly at Evil, who had retreated swiftly to a raised stone block in the middle of the room.

Then out of the darkness came a cry of 'Kevin!' And a company of mounted, full armoured knights cantered into the hall with Strutter at their head. Wheeling, their horses' hooves striking sparks from the marble floors, the knights arrayed themselves at Kevin's side, faced Evil and, as one, levelled their glittering lances in a deadly row.

'Strutter,' Kevin began, but then a strange whining noise filled the colossal hall, and down from its heights whirred a futuristic craft bristling with laser guns. Wally, at the controls, manoeuvred it to a hovering position only inches above the floor, and then smartly whipped it around to face Evil, who stood silently with his arms folded high on his chest.

Before Kevin could quite take this in, there was a rattle of gunfire, and a posse of cowboys galloped into the hall, shooting into the air and whooping and hollering like banshees. In their midst was Vermin, desperately trying to control his bucking bronco. At the same time, a phalanx of Greek archers appeared on balconies high on the marble walls, drew their bowstrings tight and aimed their long arrows at Evil's armoured breast. With them was Fidgit.

With a withering smile, Evil surveyed the forces massed against him. 'Is this the best that the Supreme Being can do?' he asked disdainfully.

Spurring his big mount, the leader of the cowboys asked Kevin: 'Is this the varmit that's been causing all the ruckus? Well, we won't have no trouble here. Come on, buckaroos. . .'

'Yahoo!' cried the cowboys, and spurring their horses they charged towards Evil with whoops and hollers, spreading their lassos as they rode. One by one the ropes snaked out and fell over Evil's head and shoulders until he was completely bound by the ropes leading out from him to the mounted cowboys like the spokes of a great wheel. Evil, not resisting at all, stared out at his mounted foes.

'You see, sonny,' called the cowboy leader, 'no problem. You can call off these other bohunks. We've got this feller all –'

But as the cowboy spoke, Evil slowly began to spin, and one by one, the riders were whipped off their horses and spun at the end of their lassos like aeroplanes on a funfair ride.

'What in tarnation!' cried their leader.

Faster and faster the helpless cowboys spun at the end of their ropes until the top of Evil's head hinged open, and a viciously sharp knife came out on a long arm and stuck itself down among the whirling ropes. One by one, the lassos snapped, and, like bullets, the cowboys flew up and out of the gaping hole in the ceiling.

'Heyyyyyyyyyyyyyyyyyyyyyyyyyyyyyyyyyy!' cried the final cowboy as he disappeared into space.

Evil stopped spinning, shrugged off the several lassos and laughed wickedly. Angrily, Kevin motioned to Strutter, and the knights spurred their great horses towards Evil, deadly lances at the ready. Calmly, Evil removed a gas mask from his robes and put it over his face. Then he threw his arms upwards in a V, and thick black smoke jetted from the flowing sleeves of his robe.

The knights, uttering wild cries, disappeared into the thick smoke.

From the blackness of the smoke came the horrific sound of clashing metal, neighing horses, and determined shouts as the knights set about Evil with all their might. Then, suddenly, all was silence. Kevin and the dwarves leaned forward expectantly, and then from the depths of the smoke veered a riderless horse, then another – and another. Finally the smoke lifted, revealing Evil unscathed and in front of him a horribly tangled mass of knights all impaled on each others' lances and quite dead. Evil smiled as if inviting them all to admire his handiwork.

Instinctively, Vermin barked a command to his Greek archers, and a deadly rain of arrows shot towards Evil. But before they could reach their target, Evil swirled his red cape around him with a defiant sweep, and it became a giant red pincushion. The archers' arrows thumped harmlessly into the cushioned surface. Then, with a great grunt, Evil expelled the arrows from the pincushion, sending them back where they came from. The archers fell, mortally pierced by their own arrows.

Finally, Kevin ordered the Sherman tank and the laser gun to fire on Evil, but with a deft wave of his hand, Evil turned the machines against the Time Bandits. The turret of the tank spun around and around firing wildly and hitting the laser craft, causing Wally to crash-land in the middle of the hall, still firing his laser cannon.

Then, totally out of Randall's control, the great tank rumbled directly towards Kevin, firing as it went. 'Look out!' cried Randall, but it was too late. The tank was nearly upon Kevin when Fidgit hurled himself forward, pushing the boy clear. Fidgit fell safely between the huge treads of the tank, but then Evil deflected a shot from Wally's laser cannon to a stone column which fell, completely crushing Fidgit.

Stunned, Kevin and the remaining dwarves ran to the fallen column, and vainly tried to lift it off Fidgit, but it was too late. 'Fidgit,' called Wally softly, and Og put his arm around Wally's shoulders to comfort him. The Time Bandits were so distraught at Fidgit's death that they nearly forgot about Evil. But his nasty, cackling laugh brought them back to reality.

Standing on the raised block of stone, Evil seemed to be growing in stature as he concentrated to summon all of his malign powers to destroy the Time Bandits. In fascination, the Time Bandits watched helplessly as Evil raised both of his arms for the final blow. Only Wally, reckless of his own safety, rushed towards Evil: 'I'll kill you, you murdering scum! Fidgit was my friend – for four thousand years – like a brother. I'll. . .'

Ignorning Wally, Evil extended his right hand towards the Time Bandits, and his entire body convulsed with power as the killing force moved from his shoulders down his arms towards his splayed fingertips.

But then, from somewhere behind the Time Bandits, a colossal bolt of lightning split the heavy air and struck Evil dead centre. He was instantly turned to pure carbon, a perfect replica of his former self in shiny black coal, petrified for the rest of time. Kevin and the dwarves turned around slowly to see what had saved them, and found themselves looking into the spectral image of the Supreme Being! Their relief was touched by fear: he had finally caught up with them.

Throwing himself to the floor before the spectral presence, Randall cried to the others: 'Down! Down! Beg for your lives!'

But then, before their wondering eyes, the Supreme Being began to change. The figure with the flowing robes and long white beard faded away, and left in his place was an elderly gent in an ill-fitting business suit, carrying a furled umbrella. His mild-mannered face was creased with worry lines, and dandruff speckled the collar of his slightly rumpled coat.

'Oh, I do hate having to appear like that,' said the

Supreme Being in a mild, slightly complaining voice. 'It really is the most tiresome and noisy manifestation. Still, it is rather expected of one, I'm afraid.'

Randall was still flat on his face and urging the others to join him. 'Get down,' he cried. 'Don't you see? It's Him!'

'Oh, do stop that,' the Supreme Being told Randall with annoyance.

But Randall was too far gone to listen. 'Oh, Great One, Supreme Being,' he beseeched, 'Glorious Creator without whom we would be mere scarab beetles on the dung heap of life. . .'

'Is this pig with you?' the Supreme Being asked, noticing the former Og rooting around in some refuse.

'Yes,' said Strutter. 'He *used* to be our friend Og.'

'Do you want him back?'

'Oh, yes, please!' they all chorused.

'Right,' said the Supreme Being, 'we'd better sort him out first.' He nodded in the pig's direction, and suddenly Og was standing there, looking confused and a bit sad.

'Oh,' he said, 'I was beginning to *enjoy* that.'

The Supreme Being looked fussily about him at the littered hall and said: 'If there's one thing I can't stand, it's a mess. Come on, let's get this place cleaned up a bit.'

They all hurriedly began cleaning up the debris, except for Wally, who still knelt beside the pillar which had crushed Fidgit, tears running down his broad face.

'Come *on*,' said Randall impatiently. 'Give us a hand, Wally.'

But Wally just looked sadly at him and said: 'He's dead, Randall. Fidgit's dead.'

'Oh, is *that* all?' said the Supreme Being. 'Well, he doesn't get out of work *that* easily.' He snapped his fingers, the column rose, and Fidgit got up looking dazed.

'Fidgit!' cried Wally. 'You're alive.'

'Yeah,' said Fidgit. 'I think so.'

'But I killed you,' Wally insisted, 'with the laser cannon.'

'Well,' said Fidgit, feeling himself all over, 'you didn't do a very good job of it.'

'Oh, hurry up!' said the Supreme Being. 'And by the way, where's that map of mine?'

Randall rummaged around until he found the map, brushed it off lovingly and then, cringing and fawning, handed it to the Supreme Being.

'Oh sir,' Randall said, 'oh Great One. We can explain everything, honestly. We didn't *mean* to steal the map. We didn't *mean* to run away. We just. . .'

'What do you mean,' the Supreme Being demanded, 'you didn't *mean* to steal the map?'

'Well,' said Randall, 'we just sort of. . .'

'Of *course* you didn't mean to steal the map,' said the Supreme Being. 'I *let* you steal it. Did you really think I didn't know?'

'Huh?' said Randall.

'I had to have some way of testing my handiwork. I think Evil turned out rather well, don't you?' he pointed to the black replica of Evil, stuck forever in its pose.

'Excuse me?' said Randall, not understanding at all.

'Evil!' repeated the Supreme Being. 'My, you *are* a little bit thick. I thought he was really quite effective. Very impressive.' The Supreme Being reached into his briefcase and held out some brown striped pyjamas and dressing-gown. 'Now, who do these belong to?'

'Me, sir,' said Kevin, recognizing the clothes in which he'd started his adventures.

'Well, here they are,' said the Supreme Being. 'You really are the most untidy boy. Sign here.' He then held out a pen and a receipt pad.

Kevin signed, and the Supreme Being checked his signature and put the pad away.

'You mean, sir,' asked Wally, the truth just beginning to dawn on him, 'that you *knew* what was happening to us? All the time?'

'Well, of course. I *am* the Supreme Being, you know.

I'm not *entirely* dim.'

'Oh, no, sir,' said Randall hastily. 'Of course not . . . it's just that we. . .'

'I let you take the map,' said the Supreme Being deliberately, as if talking to idiots. 'I chased you just as slowly as I could and still be convincing. Quite honestly, there were times when I nearly gave up the whole test. I – oh, *do* be careful! Now see what you've done.'

Strutter and Og, while they were clearing away the carbonized remains of Evil, had tripped over Fidgit and dropped the statue, which broke into many pieces all over the floor.

'That's concentrated Evil,' the Supreme Being warned them. 'The most dangerous substance the world has ever known. One speck of that could turn you all into hermit crabs for eternity. Pick it all up right now and put it in that.' He indicated a specially constructed red pillar box. 'And don't let a single bit get away.'

Kevin and the others scurried around, picking up every bit of Evil they could find, but they failed to notice that Evil's nose had rolled behind a bit of broken stone column.

'I think that's all of it, sir,' reported Randall, taking a good look around but still not noticing the missing nose.

'Oh, good.'

Then Kevin spoke up. 'You mean you let all these people die just to test your creation?' he demanded of the Supreme Being.

'Yes, of course,' said the Supreme Being. 'You're a rather clever little chap. I was really rather pleased with the way I made you. Good workmanship,' he added, giving Kevin a pat on the head.

'But why did they have to die?' Kevin insisted.

'You might as well ask,' the Supreme Being said, a bit irritated, 'why we have to have Evil.'

'Oh, we wouldn't *dream* of asking that,' said Randall quickly.

'Yes,' said Kevin, 'why *do* we have to have Evil?'

'Ah,' said the Supreme Being, rubbing his round little chin. 'I *think* it's got to do with free will or something like that. I forget.'

'Sir,' said Randall, eager to change the subject, 'do you think we might have our jobs back?'

'Well,' said the Supreme Being, 'you certainly were appallingly bad robbers. I *should* do something frightfully show-off and vengeful to you, but I'm honestly too tired. So I think I'll just transfer you to the Undergrowth Department – bracken, small shrubs and that sort of thing – with nineteen per cent cut in salary backdated to the beginning of time. Will that do you?'

'Oh yes,' said the dwarves eagerly. 'Please . . . thank you.'

'Yes . . . well,' said the Supreme Being, 'I *am* the nice one, after all. Now, have you picked up all of that concentrated Evil? Every bit of it?'

'Yes, sir,' they all cried, unaware that Evil's nose still lay undetected.

'Right. Come on then,' said the Supreme Being, 'back to Creation with you all. I mustn't waste any more time. Everyone will think I've lost control again, and start putting it all down to evolution. Let's hurry, now.'

'Sir?' said Fidgit.

'What is it?' the Supreme Being asked testily.

'What about our friend?' he indicated Kevin. 'Can he come with us?'

'Of course not,' said the Supreme Being. 'This isn't a school outing, you know.'

'But sir,' Fidgit insisted, 'we don't want to leave Kevin. Why, without him, we'd have never. . .'

'Oh, don't go on about it,' said the Supreme Being. 'Kevin has to stay here to carry on the fight, and that's all there is to it. Come on, all of you!'

Before Kevin's eyes, he changed again into the bearded figure in the flowing gown, and the glow around him both dazzled Kevin and swallowed up the Time Bandits. The glow grew until it was an all-encompassing ball of light, from the middle of which came an exasperated voice: 'Oh, I do hate this sort of thing.'

'Wait,' said Kevin with alarm. 'Please don't leave me! Please. . .'

But the noise of a rushing wind rose, and the blinding light caused Kevin to cringe back as the Supreme Being carried the Time Bandits away. 'Good-bye, Kevin,' came their voices. 'Good-bye . . . good luck.' And they were gone.

'Don't leave me,' Kevin cried. 'Don't leave me!'

Unseen by Kevin, the last remaining bit of Evil, hidden behind the fallen column, began to exude a thick black smoke which rose up all around the boy, and he began to choke and scream.

—16—
THE END

It really was impossible for Kevin to breath as the black smoke welled up on all sides. 'Help!' he cried. 'Come back! Randall, come back. Save me!'

Just then he heard somewhere the shattering crack of an axe splitting wood. He looked up. An axe shattered the door, and a horrible, bug-faced creature came through the thick smoke and leaned over Kevin. Huge eyes dominated its head, and a coiled tube where its nose should have been led into a squat canister. The creature was dressed entirely in black-streaked yellow, and the emblem on its bell-shaped helmet said 'Metropolitan Fire Brigade'.

'Come along then, sonny,' said the fireman in a muffled voice from beneath his oxygen mask, and he reached down and scooped Kevin up. As the fireman did so Kevin realized he was lying in his own bed. The fireman turned to carry Kevin towards the bedroom door, his heavy rubber boot crushing the boy's draughts board lying half folded on the floor. Around the black and white draughts board were scattered a toy tank, a laser gun and a jumbled variety of toy cowboys, knights and Greek archers.

When the fireman carried Kevin out of the front door, two fire engines were parked at angles to the street, and the blue, revolving light on a panda car flickered eerily across the faces of the small crowd of neighbours in night-clothes who stood chatting and discussing the price of electric appliances. Thick yellow hoses snaked from the fire hydrant to the Lotterbys' front door.

'I'm going back in there, Trevor,' Kevin's mother insisted hysterically, straining towards the still-smoking maisonette.

'Don't be a fool, Diane,' Kevin's father said, trying to hold her back. 'Kevin is out now. He's okay.'

'I'm going back in for the toaster,' she cried, struggling against his superior strength. 'It's brand new!'

At one of the fire engines, the fireman who saved Kevin sat him down on the big leather front seat. 'Are you okay?' he asked, pulling off his oxygen mask to reveal a face heavily grimed with greasy smoke.

'Sure, I think so,' Kevin said, looking around in wonder at the scene around him. 'But I thought for a moment . . .' he let his voice trail off to nothing.

'Okay, you just sit here for a while and get your breath,' said the fireman, turning away to return to the front door of the Lotterbys' house where other firemen were clearing up, carrying rolled-up hoses back to the engines and preparing to leave. He disappeared into the house.

But in a few minutes, the fireman was back carrying a scorched microwave oven in his arms.

'If you were half a man,' Mrs Lotterby was shouting at her husband, 'you'd have gone in there and saved the blender!'

'This is where it started,' the fireman told Kevin's parents, setting the blackened microwave oven down on the grass in front of them.

'My Supermicrotonic oven!' Mrs Lotterby cried, falling on her knees in front of the ruined appliance.

As the fireman walked towards the other fire engine, someone handed him a towel, and he wiped his smoke-smeared face as he climbed in. Suddenly, Kevin saw the fireman's face clearly for the first time, and he recognized him.

'Agamemnon!' Kevin cried, jumping down to the ground and starting towards the other fire engine. But by that time it was beginning to pull away from the kerb. The fireman sitting in the passenger's seat turned his head and looked Kevin full in the face. It *was* Agamemnon. And as the fire engine gathered speed, he gave Kevin a broad wink and a thumb's-up sign. Then he was gone.

Slightly dazed, Kevin turned back to his parents, who were kneeling around the microwave oven, bickering.

'Well, *I* certainly didn't leave it in there,' Mrs Lotterby protested.

'Who does the cooking, eh?' Mr Lotterby demanded. 'Not *me*, certainly.'

'It's been *years* since I cooked a joint,' Mrs Lotterby protested. 'I've practically forgotten how.'

'What do you call *this*, then?' Mr Lotterby asked triumphantly, pointing at the open oven. There, sitting on the rack, was a small piece of black substance which just *might* have been the charred remains of a joint left in the microwave oven for far too long. But with horror Kevin recognized it as Evil's carbonized nose which had evaded the dwarves' clean-up of the great hall. He recalled vividly the Supreme Being saying: 'That's concentrated Evil, the most dangerous substance the world has ever known.'

'Dad! Mum!' Kevin cried to try to warn them.

'Here, I'll show you,' Kevin's father was saying as he reached into the oven to grasp the black substance.

'No, Dad,' Kevin shouted. 'Don't!'

But it was too late.

THE END
(Or is it?)

THE SPARROW BOOK OF RECORD-BREAKERS

Pamela Cleaver

Children have flown planes in the RAF, ridden in cavalry charges and formed an army in which the eldest soldier was twelve years old. A young boy was used as a spy in World War Two, and the youngest author to have a book published was only four and a half years old.

And that is only the beginning . . .

85p

THE SPUDDY

Lillian Beckwith

He was a grey-black mongrel; tough, canny, loyal – and abandoned. The fishermen called him The Spuddy.

The only person to care for The Spuddy in the busy Hebridean village of Gaymal is Andy, a young, dumb boy staying in the town with relatives. For both of them, their meeting brings friendship after loneliness; but when the new companions are taken up by Jake, skipper of the *Silver Crest*, events take a swift and unexpected turn.

85p

MIDSHIPMAN BOLITHO AND THE 'AVENGER'

Alexander Kent

December 1773
Midshipman Bolitho's ship, the *Gorgon*, is laid up in Falmouth for refitting, and the young sailor – now seventeen – looks forward to a peaceful Christmas with his family.

But Cornwall is now a violent place. Smuggling is rife, witchcraft abounds, and ugly rumours lead to the murder of a revenue officer. As the *Gorgon* lies helplessly in dry dock, piracy and wrecking become a dangerous threat to the undefended shores.

Then one day the *Avenger*, a small man-of-war, sails into Falmouth, captained by Richard Bolitho's brother; and before long the young midshipman is embroiled in a fierce and bloody struggle for domination of the seas.

80p